Eruptions of Popular Anger

Eruptions of Popular Anger

The Economics of the Arab Spring and Its Aftermath

Elena Ianchovichina

MENA Development Report Series

This series features major development reports from the Middle East and North Africa region of the World Bank, based on new research and thoroughly peer-reviewed analysis. Each report aims to enrich the debate on the main development challenges and opportunities the region faces as it strives to meet the evolving needs of its people.

Titles in the MENA Development Report Series

Privilege-Resistant Policies in the Middle East and North Africa: Measurement and Operational Implications (2018) by Syed Akhtar Mahmood and Meriem Ait Ali Slimane

Eruptions of Popular Anger: The Economics of the Arab Spring and Its Aftermath (2018) by Elena Ianchovichina

Beyond Scarcity: Water Security in the Middle East and North Africa (2018) by World Bank

Jobs or Privileges: Unleashing the Employment Potential of the Middle East and North Africa (2015) by Marc Schiffbauer, Abdoulaye Sy, Sahar Hussain, Hania Sahnoun, and Philip Keefer

The Road Traveled: Dubai's Journey towards Improving Private Education: A World Bank Review (2014) by Simon Thacker and Ernesto Cuadra

Inclusion and Resilience: The Way Forward for Social Safety Nets in the Middle East and North Africa (2013) by Joana Silva, Victoria Levin, and Matteo Morgandi

Opening Doors: Gender Equality and Development in the Middle East and North Africa (2013) by World Bank

From Political to Economic Awakening in the Arab World: The Path of Economic Integration (2013) by Jean-Pierre Chauffour

Adaptation to a Changing Climate in the Arab Countries: A Case for Adaptation Governance and Leadership in Building Climate Resilience (2012) by Dorte Verner

Renewable Energy Desalination: An Emerging Solution to Close the Water Gap in the Middle East and North Africa (2012) by World Bank

Poor Places, Thriving People: How the Middle East and North Africa Can Rise Above Spatial Disparities (2011) by World Bank

Financial Access and Stability: A Road Map for the Middle East and North Africa (2011) by Roberto R. Rocha, Zsofia Arvai, and Subika Farazi

From Privilege to Competition: Unlocking Private-Led Growth in the Middle East and North Africa (2009) by World Bank

The Road Not Traveled: Education Reform in the Middle East and North Africa (2008) by World Bank

Making the Most of Scarcity: Accountability for Better Water Management Results in the Middle East and North Africa (2007) by World Bank

Gender and Development in the Middle East and North Africa: Women in the Public Sphere (2004) by World Bank

Unlocking the Employment Potential in the Middle East and North Africa: Toward a New Social Contract (2004) by World Bank

Better Governance for Development in the Middle East and North Africa: Enhancing Inclusiveness and Accountability (2003) by World Bank

Trade, Investment and Development in the Middle East and North Africa: Engaging with the World (2003) by World Bank

All books in the MENA Development Report series are available for free at https://openknowledge.worldbank.org/handle /10986/2168.

Contents

Acknowledgments

This report was written by Elena Ianchovichina with inputs from Nadia Belhaj Hassine, Roy van der Weide, Christoph Lakner, and Niels Johannesen on economic inequality; Hai-anh Dang on welfare dynamics with synthetic panels; Martijn Burger, Efstratia Arampatzi, and Caroline Witte on subjective well-being and protests; Shantayanan Devarajan on the social contract; Suleiman Abu Bader on conflict, polarization, and external military interventions; and Youssouf Kiendrebeogo on perceptions and violent extremism.

The work was led by Elena Ianchovichina and was conducted under the general guidance of Shantayanan Devarajan, Chief Economist of the World Bank's Middle East and North Africa (MENA) Region. Guoliang Feng assisted the team with urban house price data for the Arab Republic of Egypt; Tina Röhricht worked with the Gallup World Poll data; Youssouf Kiendrebeogo worked with the household surveys, the Gallup World Poll data, and the data on wealth; Stylianos Michalopoulos provided information on spatial and ethnic inequality; and Rayah Al-Farah and Nathaniel Reilly reviewed different strands of the political economy literature in the context of the Arab Spring and political violence.

We received valuable comments on the background papers and notes for this report during a workshop on the Arab Inequality Puzzle, organized by the World Bank's MENA Chief Economist's Office in April 2015 in Washington, DC; the International Association for Research in Income and Wealth–Central Agency for Public Mobilization and Statistics Conference "Experiences and Challenges in Measuring Income, Wealth, Poverty and Inequality in the Middle East and North Africa" in November 2015 in Cairo, Egypt; the 11th Defence and Security Economics Workshop in November 2016 at Carleton University, Ottawa, Canada; the Northeast Universities Development Consortium (NEUDC) Conference 2016 at the MIT Sloan School of Management, Cambridge, MA; the Centre for the Study of African Economies Conference 2015 at

St. Catherine's College, University of Oxford, U.K.; the 37th Annual Meeting of the Middle East Economic Association (MEEA) in Chicago, IL; the Organisation for Economic Co-operation and Development– World Bank Conference "The Squeezed Middle Class in OECD and Emerging Countries—Myth and Reality" in December 2016, Paris, France; and the National Bureau of Economic Research Meeting "Economics of National Security" in March 2017, Boston, MA.

At the early stages of this work, the team was fortunate to receive comments from Francisco Ferreira, Martin Ravallion, Ana Revenga, Ravi Kanbur, Aart Kraay, Marcelo Giugale, Peter Lanjouw, Caroline Freund, Branko Milanovic, Quy-Toan Do, Martin Rama, Paolo Verme, Sami Bibi, and Hadi Esfahani. The team received useful comments at the final stages of this work from peer reviewers François Bourguignon and Edouard Al-Dahdah, and from Bledi Celiku; and at the concept-note stage from peer reviewers Carol Graham and Ellen Lust, and from Tara Vishwanath, Najy Benhassine, Deborah Wetzel, and Gabriel Ibarra. The final manuscript was reviewed by Ravi Kanbur. The team would like to acknowledge financial support for the background papers commissioned for this study from the U.K. Department for International Development through its Strategic Research Program.

About the Author and Contributors

Elena Ianchovichina is a lead economist in the Office of the Chief Economist of the World Bank's Middle East and North Africa Region, where on many occasions she has served as the acting regional chief economist. Since joining the World Bank in 2000, she has been a young professional in the Development Research Group and the East Asia and Pacific Region and an economist and a senior economist in the Economic Policy and Debt Department, where she managed the program on inclusive growth. Her research covers a wide range of topics in development and international economics, including trade policy, economic growth, foreign investment, global general equilibrium modeling, natural resources, food security, inequality, and political violence. She is the author or coauthor of numerous publications, and her work has been published in academic journals, including the *World Bank Economic Review*, *World Development*, the *Journal of International Business Studies*, *Ecological Economics*, the *Review of Income and Wealth*, and the *Journal of Development Studies*. Born in Bulgaria, Ms. Ianchovichina received her PhD from Purdue University in Indiana.

Suleiman Abu-Bader is an associate professor in the Department of Economics of Ben-Gurion University of the Negev, Israel. His research interests are currently focused on the factors explaining the differences in income inequality levels and their changes for the Palestinian Arabs in Israel and the West Bank and Gaza and the relationships among polarization, external military intervention, and civil conflict. He has published his research in academic journals, including *World Development*, the *Review of International Economics*, and *Applied Economics*. Mr. Abu-Bader holds a PhD in economics from Cornell University, an MA in economics from Ben-Gurion University of the Negev, and a BA in mathematics and statistics from the Hebrew University of Jerusalem.

Efstratia Arampatzi is a researcher and PhD candidate at the Erasmus Happiness Economics Research Organization at Erasmus University

Rotterdam. Her research focuses on happiness economics and the determinants of subjective well-being, including the effects of economic shocks and the role of governance, occupational choice, and social network sites. She has coauthored several articles published in the *Journal of Happiness Studies* and *Applied Economic Letters*. Ms. Arampatzi holds a degree in international and European studies from University of Macedonia in Greece and a master's degree in economics and business from Erasmus University in the Netherlands.

Martijn Burger is the Academic Director at the Erasmus Happiness Economics Research Organization and an associate professor of industrial and regional economics in the Department of Applied Economics at Erasmus University Rotterdam. Most of his current research focuses on happiness economics and urban and regional economics, including geography of happiness, location decisions of multinational corporations, and institutional and social conditions for economic development. In addition, he is associate director of the Globalization and World Cities Network, associate editor of the *Journal of Economic and Social Geography*, and a member of the boards of the Dutch Regional Science Association and the International Society for Quality of Life Studies. Mr. Burger obtained his PhD in economics from Erasmus University Rotterdam.

Hai-Anh H. Dang is an economist in the Survey Unit of the World Bank's Development Data Group. His research on poverty, education, labor, and other economic development topics has been published in leading development journals, including the *Journal of Development Economics*, the *World Bank Economic Review*, the *Review of Income and Wealth*, the *European Journal of Political Economy*, and *Economic Development and Cultural Change*. He has received research grants from the Hewlett Foundation and the UK Department for International Development. Mr. Dang earned his BA from Foreign Trade University in Vietnam and his PhD in applied economics from the University of Minnesota.

Shantayanan Devarajan is the Senior Director for Development Economics at the World Bank. Previously, he was the Chief Economist of the World Bank's Middle East and North Africa Region. Since joining the World Bank in 1991, he has been a principal economist and the Research Manager for Public Economics in the Development Research Group, and the Chief Economist of the Human Development Network, the South Asia Region, and the Africa Region. He was a director of the *World Development Report 2004, Making Services Work for Poor People*. Before 1991, he was on the faculty of Harvard University's John F. Kennedy School of Government. Mr. Devarajan is the author or coauthor of more than 100 publications, and his research covers public economics, trade policy, natural resources and the environment, and general equilibrium modeling of developing countries. Born in Sri Lanka,

Mr. Devarajan received his BA in mathematics from Princeton University and his PhD in economics from the University of California, Berkeley.

Nadia Belhaj Hassine is a senior economist in the World Bank's Africa Poverty Global Practice covering Tanzania, Burundi, Sudan, Comoros, and Madagascar. Before joining the World Bank, she was a senior program specialist with the Canada International Development Research Center. She has also taught at many universities, including the University of Toulouse in France and the University of Nabeul in Tunisia. Her research areas are poverty and inequality, agricultural economics, and applied econometrics. She has published many articles in academic journals including *World Development*, the *World Bank Economic Review*, the *European Review of Agricultural Economics*, and the *Journal of Development Studies*.

Niels Johannesen is an associate professor in the Department of Economics, University of Copenhagen. Much of his research revolves around offshore tax evasion, including a recent paper that combines customer data leaked from offshore intermediaries with tax returns to quantify the implications of hidden wealth for wealth inequality. He has published in journals such as the *American Economic Review*, the *Journal of the European Economic Association*, the *American Economic Journal: Economic Policy*, the *Journal of International Economics*, and the *Journal of Public Economics*.

Youssouf Kiendrebeogo is an economist in the Office of the Chief Economist of the World Bank's Middle East and North Africa Region. He joined the Bank in 2014, after earning his PhD and MS in economics from the University of Auvergne (CERDI) in France. His research focuses on open economy macroeconomics, trade policy, financial development, growth, and inequality. Before joining the Bank, he worked as a research fellow at the International Monetary Fund and taught econometrics at the University of Auvergne.

Christoph Lakner is an economist in the Poverty and Inequality Unit of the World Bank's Development Research Group. He previously worked in the World Bank's Poverty Global Practice on poverty and inequality issues in Argentina. His research interests include inequality, poverty, and labor markets in developing countries, with a special emphasis on global inequality, the relationship between inequality of opportunity and growth, the implications of regional price differences for inequality, and the income composition of top incomes. He holds a BA, MPhil, and DPhil in economics from the University of Oxford.

Roy van der Weide is an economist in the Poverty and Inequality Research team within the World Bank's Development Research Group. He recently assumed the responsibility of leading the poverty and inequality mapping research within the department. His other research is concerned with the empirics of inequality of opportunity and poverty reduction, axiomatic approaches to income measurement, spatial econometrics, and the transmission of price inflation and volatility. His work has been published in a range of academic journals including the *American Economic Review*, the *Journal of Econometrics*, the *Journal of Applied Econometrics*, and the *World Bank Economic Review*. He holds a PhD from the University of Amsterdam.

Caroline Witte is an assistant professor of International Business at the Copenhagen Business School and a PhD candidate at the Erasmus School of Economics and the Erasmus Institute of Management at Erasmus University Rotterdam. Her research interests include political conflict, political risk management, firm location decisions, and economic geography. She has published in the *Journal of International Business Studies*, and her dissertation proposal was awarded the 2016 Sheth/AIB dissertation proposal award.

Abbreviations

BIS	Bank for International Settlements
DMNA	Developing Middle East and North Africa
EAP	East Asia and Pacific
ECA	Europe and Central Asia
GCC	Gulf Cooperation Council
GDP	gross domestic product
HICs	high-income countries
LAC	Latin America and the Caribbean
LMICs	low- and middle-income countries
MENA	Middle East and North Africa
OECD	Organisation for Economic Co-operation and Development
PPP	purchasing power parity
SAR	South Asia
SSA	Sub-Saharan Africa
VAT	value added tax

Overview

The Arab Spring protests caught most of the world by surprise[1] and precipitated a chain of events that changed the course of history in the Middle East and North Africa (MENA), ushering in a period of prolonged political instability and intense civil conflict. On the eve of the Arab Spring, the cracks in the MENA models of government remained invisible to most observers.[2] Arab states were long-standing autocracies, viewed favorably by the West,[3] and considered to be relatively stable. Only 2 of the 18 MENA countries—Iraq and the Republic of Yemen—made it to the top of the 2010 Failed States Index published in *Foreign Policy*, and most of them earned relatively favorable political stability ratings (figure O.1).

Economic indicators tracking income growth, poverty rates, and expenditure or income inequality also presented a favorable picture and suggested that the autocratic Arab regimes had delivered on economic, human development, and shared prosperity goals. In the five-year period before the Arab Spring, annual gross domestic product (GDP) growth averaged about 4.5 percent in Tunisia, 5 percent in Morocco, and about 6 percent in Jordan, the Arab Republic of Egypt, and the Syrian Arab Republic. Economic growth in developing MENA as a whole surpassed that in Latin America and the Caribbean and in developing Europe and Central Asia (figure O.2). Less impressively, given still relatively high population growth despite declining fertility rates, per capita output grew by 3 percent, on average, during the same period, which was slightly higher than per capita output growth in Latin America and the Caribbean, but lower than that in Europe and Central Asia (figure O.2).

Poverty rates were declining in all economies except the Republic of Yemen, and absolute poverty incidence, measured at $1.25 a day, was extremely low before the Arab Spring (figure O.3). Not only did MENA reach the Millennium Development Goals related to poverty and access to infrastructure services (especially drinking water and sanitation, and Internet connectivity) but it also made important strides in reducing

FIGURE O.1

Political Instability Index, 2003–12

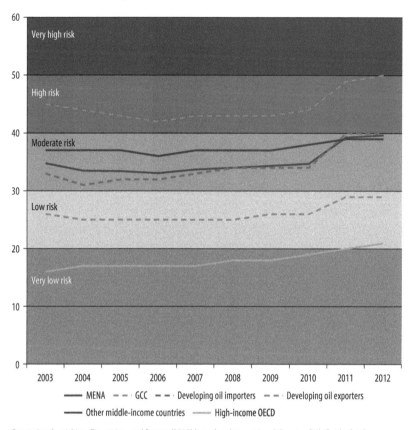

Source: Ianchovichina, Devarajan, and Burger (2013) based on International Country Risk Guide database.
Note: An increase in the index reflects an increase in political instability. MENA = Middle East and North Africa;
GCC = Gulf Cooperation Council; OECD = Organisation for Economic Co-operation and Development.

hunger and child and maternal mortality, and in increasing school enrollment (Iqbal and Kiendrebeogo 2016). Inequality of opportunity declined
in Egypt and some other MENA countries according to Hassine (2012)
and Assaad et al. (2016). Expenditure inequality, measured by the Gini
index, was either constant or declining in most MENA economies and
remained moderate by international standards (figure O.4). The incomes
of the bottom 40 percent of the population, measured as 2005 purchas-
ing-power-parity-adjusted per capita expenditure, grew faster than average expenditure[4] in most developing MENA economies for which
information was available (figure O.5). In fact, the ratio of expenditures
of the bottom 40 percent to the average was higher in MENA than in all
other developing regions except Latin America and the Caribbean. On
the basis of this information, one could have concluded that the benefits
of economic growth were broadly shared in the Arab world.

FIGURE O.2

Annual Economic Output Growth, 2005–10

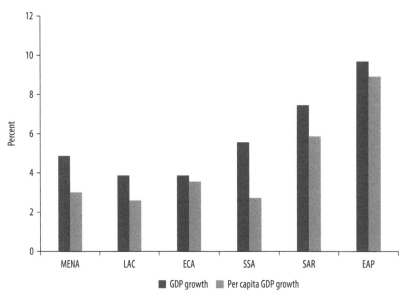

Source: World Bank, World Development Indicators.
Note: EAP = East Asia and Pacific; ECA = Europe and Central Asia; GDP = gross domestic product; LAC = Latin America and the Caribbean; MENA = Middle East and North Africa; SAR = South Asia; SSA = Sub-Saharan Africa.

FIGURE O.3

Poverty Rates

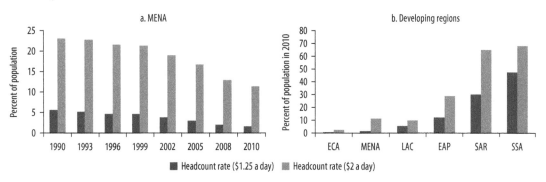

Sources: World Bank PovcalNet; World Bank data.
Note: EAP = East Asia and Pacific; ECA = Europe and Central Asia; LAC = Latin America and the Caribbean; MENA = Middle East and North Africa; SAR = South Asia; SSA = Sub-Saharan Africa.

Yet, starting in late 2010, uprisings began, first in Tunisia and then in most other developing Arab countries. The collective Arab Barometer data suggest that the typical Arab protestor was single, educated, relatively young (younger than 44), middle class, urban, and male (figure O.6). These protestors raised their voices to demand improved

FIGURE O.4

Expenditure Inequality, over Time and across the World

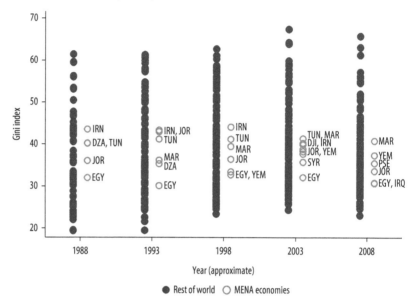

Source: Data from Lakner and Milanovic 2013.
Note: MENA = Middle East and North Africa; DJI = Djibouti; DZA = Algeria; EGY = Arab Republic of Egypt; IRN = Islamic Republic of Iran; IRQ = Iraq; JOR = Jordan; MAR = Morocco; PSE = West Bank and Gaza; SYR = Syrian Arab Republic; TUN = Tunisia; YEM = Republic of Yemen.

FIGURE O.5

Shared Prosperity

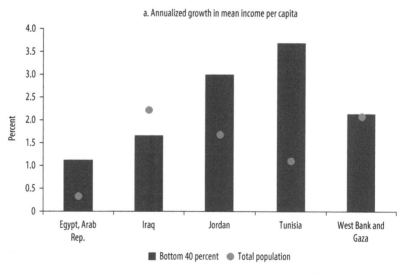

a. Annualized growth in mean income per capita

(continued on next page)

FIGURE O.5

Shared Prosperity *Continued*

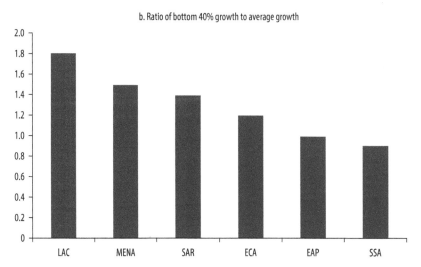

b. Ratio of bottom 40% growth to average growth

Sources: Household Survey Data; World Bank, Global Database of Shared Prosperity; World Bank, World Development Indicators.
Note: Because of data limitations, the growth rates in panel a apply to different time periods in different economies: Egypt (2005–08), Iraq (2007–12), Jordan (2006–10), Tunisia (2005–10), and West Bank and Gaza (2004–09). EAP = East Asia and Pacific; ECA = Europe and Central Asia; LAC = Latin America and the Caribbean; MENA = Middle East and North Africa; SAR = South Asia; SSA = Sub-Saharan Africa.

FIGURE O.6

Profile of the Arab Spring Protestors

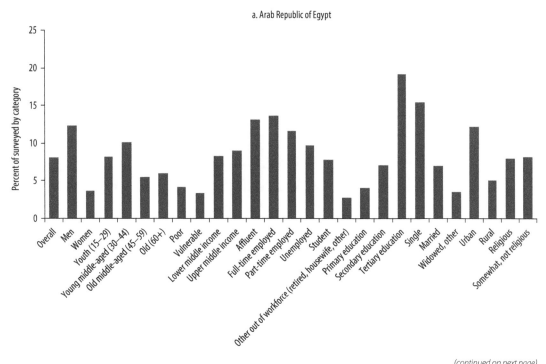

a. Arab Republic of Egypt

(continued on next page)

FIGURE O.6

Profile of the Arab Spring Protestors   *Continued*

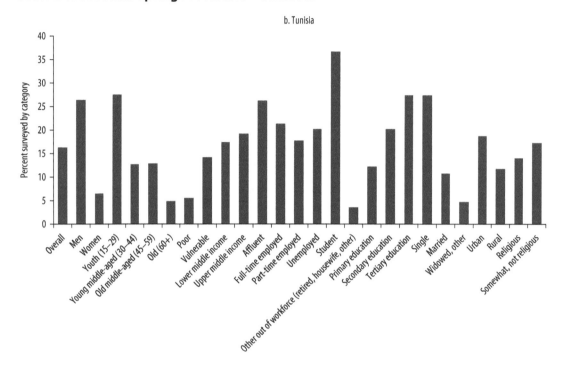

b. Tunisia

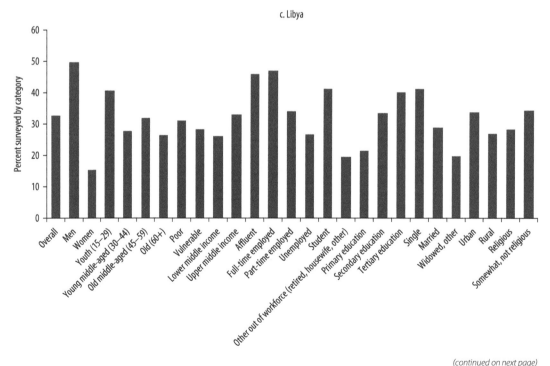

c. Libya

(continued on next page)

FIGURE O.6

Profile of the Arab Spring Protestors *Continued*

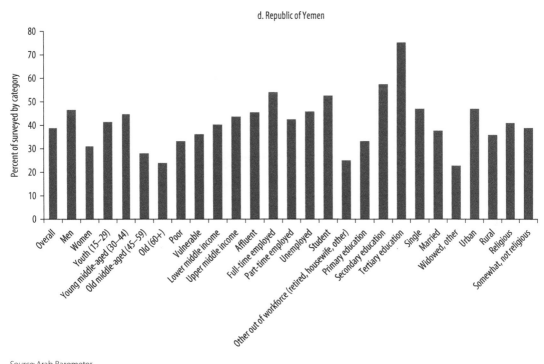

d. Republic of Yemen

Source: Arab Barometer.

economic opportunities and social and economic justice (figure O.7) and to express their dissatisfaction with corruption and deterioration in their quality of life, particularly public service quality (figure O.8).

The aftermath of the Arab Spring was a period of intense political instability and violence. In Egypt, Libya, Tunisia, and the Republic of Yemen, the uprisings overthrew long-standing authoritarian governments; in Syria, the uprising turned into an armed insurgency and eventually into a protracted civil war; there was a resurgence of armed unrest in Iraq and eventually the formation of the Islamic State of Iraq and Syria. Popular discontent was widespread in many other Arab countries, including Bahrain, Jordan, and Morocco. The uprisings' onset was unexpected—standard development indicators did not capture the brewing discontent. Once the uprisings occurred, however, issues of equity and inclusion came to the fore. In particular, income inequality was cited as one of the factors behind the Egyptian revolution (Hlasny and Verme 2016; Nimeh 2012; Ncube and Anyanwu 2012; Osborn 2011).

Three Puzzles

The idea that income inequality is linked to revolution can be traced to ancient times when social philosophers speculated that economic

FIGURE O.7

Reasons for Arab Spring Based on Views in Developing MENA

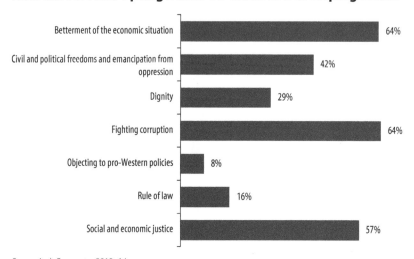

Source: Arab Barometer 2012–14.
Note: MENA = Middle East and North Africa.

FIGURE O.8

Dissatisfaction with Government Services in Arab Spring Countries

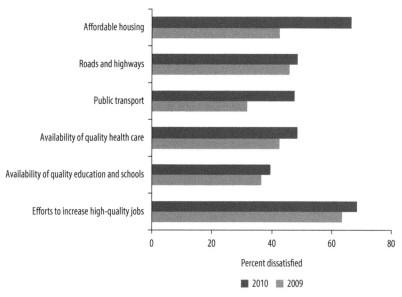

Source: Data from Gallup World Poll.

inequality was a fundamental cause of civil unrest (Muller 1985). Today, even though tolerance for income inequality varies over time and across countries (Hirschman and Rothschild 1973), high income inequality is considered bad for political stability and can be harmful to economic development in resource-rich countries (Behzadan et al. 2017). Political instability, in turn, could harm investment, sustainable growth, and progress in human development (Ostry, Berg, and Tsangarides 2014; Burger, Ianchovichina, and Rijkers 2016).

The apparent disconnect between the relatively low and mostly declining or stagnant economic inequality in the Arab world and the eruption of popular anger during the Arab Spring uprisings in 2010–11 is a puzzle. This study aims to solve this "Arab inequality" puzzle by using rigorous empirical research drawing on an eclectic mix of economic, sociological, and political data. Along the way, more paradoxes and puzzles are encountered, including the "unhappy development" paradox, described by Arampatzi et al. (2015) as declining levels of happiness during a time of moderate-to-rapid development progress. In this study it is also called the unhappy development syndrome because it captures the symptoms of a broken social contract.[5] During the Arab Spring aftermath, yet another paradox emerged, namely, the high incidence of political violence in countries that do not fit the profile of fragile states, referred to in the study as the paradox of "political violence in middle-income countries."

This study is not a comprehensive account of all factors that could have played a role in any single country, but an exploration of common factors that mattered to different degrees in all Arab countries; that is, the study picks up common regional themes. It is guided by the central question of how economic factors fit into the Arab Spring story and its aftermath. The inquiry goes beyond traditional macroeconomic and microeconomic analyses and uses data on subjective well-being and its determinants. The analysis of the Arab Spring's aftermath sheds light on the interplay between economic, behavioral, institutional, and political factors that have influenced the transitions across the region and the risk of civil conflict. The study draws on four main bodies of literature on poverty and inequality, subjective well-being, civil conflict, and macroeconomics, as well as on an eclectic mix of quantitative and qualitative methods and data. Given the complex nature of the Arab Spring and its aftermath, the study also touches on areas related to political economy and governance. The narrative is structured around the quest for answers to the three paradoxes posed above— Arab inequality, unhappy development, and political violence in middle-income countries. The volume presents empirical evidence and arguments in three parts, placing an emphasis on the demand for change in parts 1 and 2 and exploring supply-side factors that led to political change and conflict in part 3.

Part 1 introduces the Arab inequality puzzle and explores in depth poverty and inequality trends and welfare dynamics in Arab states during the decades preceding the Arab Spring. The question of whether popular anger has been growing in response to rising inequality or a middle-class squeeze is important because, depending on the answer, different remedies would be appropriate. Chapter 1, "Economic Inequality: Measurement and Biases," covers distributional concerns related to the degree of economic inequality and discusses new data and techniques introduced to deal with data gaps and measurement biases. Given the absence of empirical evidence of high and rising inequality, chapter 2, "Welfare Dynamics: Definitions and Measurement," defines the middle class in the Arab context and turns to analysis of intragenerational welfare mobility (mobility across welfare classes within generations).

Part 2 provides an answer to the Arab inequality puzzle by examining the reasons behind the decline in subjective well-being before the Arab Spring. Chapter 3, "Dissatisfaction with Life: Subjective Data Analysis," discusses the concept of life satisfaction and compares it with monetary-based welfare measures; the chapter relies on value surveys to track the evolution of subjective well-being levels in Arab countries before the Arab Spring. Chapter 4, "Subjective Well-Being Dynamics," presents evidence on the unhappy development paradox in the pre–Arab Spring period. The rise of dissatisfaction rates, particularly in Arab Spring countries,[6] signals that demand for change was strongest in Egypt, Syria, Tunisia, and the Republic of Yemen. In chapter 5, "Symptoms of a Broken Social Contract," the major grievances negatively associated with life satisfaction are linked with the symptoms of a broken social contract. The chapter discusses the role of economic exclusion and other policies in the breakdown of the contract.

Part 3 turns to the Arab Spring's aftermath, a period interspersed with transitional recessions, economic crises, intense political instability, and in some cases, large-scale civil conflicts. Chapter 6, "Arab Spring Protestors and Protests," presents a profile of protestors and the characteristics of the protests and riots. Chapter 7, "The Aftermath of the Arab Spring," discusses the factors that played a stabilizing role and those that turned armed insurgencies into large-scale civil wars, giving rise to the paradox of political violence in middle-income countries. Chapter 8, "Development Consequences and Policy Implications," discusses the consequences of political violence and the broad implications of the empirical findings.

Summary of Findings

The study rules out high and rising inequality as a reason for the Arab Spring uprisings. It finds that expenditure inequality in most Arab countries was low to moderate in the years before the uprisings (Hassine 2014), although it may have been substantially underestimated in the data because of missing top incomes, as shown for Egypt (van der Weide, Lakner, and Ianchovichina, forthcoming) and other countries around the world (Atkinson, Piketty, and Saez 2011). Wealth concentration in publicly traded companies also did not appear to be higher in MENA than elsewhere in the world, and the gap between MENA's and other regions' foreign tax haven bank deposits, represented as a share of GDP, had disappeared over the course of the previous two decades (Johannesen 2015). In an important development, expenditure inequality declined during the 2000s in Tunisia and Egypt, the two countries where the Arab Spring revolutions first took place (Hassine 2014). An analysis of welfare dynamics during the years preceding the uprising suggests that the real problem had been erosion of middle-class incomes (Dang and Ianchovichina 2016), which either declined or lagged behind incomes of other welfare groups (table O.1). The middle class was getting squeezed and the middle-class consensus was eroding, especially in the Arab Spring countries.

The second part of the study provides clues to solving the Arab inequality puzzle by exploring alternative measures of welfare that capture people's views about their well-being. On the eve of the Arab Spring, people felt stuck. The middle class, in particular, was growing more frustrated

TABLE O.1

Annual Growth in Mean Consumption, by Income Group before 2010

percent

Country/economy	Bottom 40%	Middle 40%	Top 20%
Syrian Arab Republic	14.9	5.7	31.5
Tunisia	5.1	2.4	−5.4
West Bank and Gaza	3.8	−0.3	2.2
Jordan	2.0	−0.7	−2.8
Egypt, Arab Rep.	−4.0	−1.6	−1.5
Yemen, Rep.	−10.3	−3.8	17.3
Average	1.9	0.3	6.3

Source: Dang and Ianchovichina 2016.
Note: The 40th and 80th percentiles of the income distribution in the first period are used as the thresholds that, respectively, identify the bottom 40 percent and the middle 40 percent of the population for both periods. The period length varies across countries and refers to the period 1997–2004 for Syria, 1998–2006 for the Republic of Yemen, 2004–09 for Egypt, 2006–08 for Jordan, and 2005–10 for Tunisia.

with the quality of life in their countries. Life satisfaction scores declined markedly before the Arab Spring events, especially for the middle class in the Arab Spring countries. Arampatzi et al. (2015) associate this unhappy development with perceptions of declining standards of living, especially the deteriorating quality of public services and labor market conditions, and the growing dissatisfaction with corruption linked to the inability of people to do well without *wasta*, that is, connections with powerful political and business elites, particularly in the Arab Spring countries. These grievances negatively affected life satisfaction and were symptoms of a broken social contract.

The grievances of the populations are linked to Gurr's (1970) "relative deprivation" theory and the broken social contract. The social contract between Arab governments and citizens that had persisted since independence consisted of the state's providing jobs in the public sector, free education and health, and subsidized food and fuel to all citizens. In return for the state's largesse, citizens were expected to keep their voices low and to tolerate some level of elite capture. Because the social contracts were kept in place through coercion, and exclusion generated anger about relative deprivation between the connected and those without connections, a breakdown in the social contract increased the premium on freedom and created impetus for political change.[7] Thus, a broken social contract, not high inequality, led to the Arab Spring uprisings.

Starting in the 2000s, evidence of the cracks in the social contracts in developing MENA began to mount. The contracts had become unsustainable because persistent fiscal imbalances emerged. The public sector could no longer be the employer of choice, and the system of general energy and food subsidies had become a fiscal burden. Therefore, reforms were passed to limit the growth of public sector employment and reduce the cost of subsidies (Devarajan and Ianchovichina 2017). Young people could no longer count on public employment after graduating from college. But the private sector did not generate enough jobs to absorb the large number of young people entering the labor force. The combination of a significant decline in child mortality and relatively slow onset of the decline in fertility in the region led to a rapid increase in the proportion of youth between the ages of 15 and 24, the so-called youth bulge (Assaad and Roudi-Fahimi 2007).

The propensity of private firms to create high-quality jobs was impeded by distortions and elite capture (Schiffbauer et al. 2015; Rijkers, Freund, and Nucifora 2017). Energy subsidies biased production in favor of capital-intensive activities, limiting the job-creating effect of economic growth; and elite capture tilted the business environment in favor of the connected few. The private sector was weakened by regulations that limited firm entry and domestic competition and cultivated a culture of

TABLE O.2

Evidence of Elite Capture in Tunisia: Ben Ali Family's Share
percent of respective total for Tunisia in 2010

Wage workers	Output	Net profits	Gross profits	Firms
1.7	5.3	15.8	10.8	0.2

Source: Rijkers, Freund, and Nucifora 2017.

rent-seeking, corruption, and cronyism. A few large, connected, old domestic firms dominated local markets for years and earned rents through monopoly power (see table O.2 for Tunisia) that allowed them to charge higher prices for their goods and services (Rijkers, Freund, and Nucifora 2017). Under the protection of regulations, large domestic companies did not have incentives to invest to compete, expand market share, and innovate.

The services sectors were particularly exposed to elite capture. They remained closed to competition (Hoekman and Sekkat 2009), and the high prices and poor quality of domestic services hurt the competitiveness of firms in other sectors, particularly of those exporting goods to global markets. Uncompetitive currencies (Freund and Jaud 2015), political instability (Burger, Ianchovichina, and Rijkers 2016), and inequitable distribution of resource rents (Behzadan et al. 2017) created Dutch disease dynamics, hurting the tradables sectors in many MENA countries. Production in the offshore sector remained skewed toward low-value-added, assembly-type operations; and the sector did not create many good-quality jobs or spillovers to other sectors in the domestic economy. Elite capture cost significant fiscal resources because the state could not generate sufficient tax revenues from the weak private sector.

As a result, the MENA region overall had some of the highest unemployment rates in the developing world, especially for youth. The quality of available jobs in the private sector was also not as good as that of jobs in the public sector. Moreover, while education and health care were free, and energy and water were subsidized, the quality of these services was so poor that many people turned to the private sector for them. People felt that they needed connections to those in power to obtain good-quality jobs, and many expressed concern that they could not move ahead no matter how hard they worked (Arampatzi et al. 2015).

At the end of 2010, Arab people started raising their voices in protest against governments that had not kept their part of the social bargain. Once mass protests sparked the political transition in Tunisia, contagion to the rest of the region was quick, enabled by technology and common language; but it mostly reflected that the economic problems and popular grievances were common throughout the developing parts of the MENA region. Consistent with Gurr's (1970) relative deprivation theory, the protestors, who were mostly middle-class young people, were frustrated about the discrepancy between their expectations and reality and the limited opportunities for personal growth and change in Arab economies and society. Better educated than their parents, young people expected to do better than the previous generation but instead struggled to find good-quality jobs. Jobless young men could not hope to get married without a stable source of income (Bromley 2014). Huge progress in reducing and, in some cases, eliminating gender gaps in education, and declines in fertility rates, suggested that Arab women were more prepared than ever to participate in the labor market and contribute to economic life. The reality, however, was that unemployment rates among women were much higher than those among men, and female labor force participation rates remained low (Devarajan and Ianchovichina 2017).

Few people foresaw the gravity of the events that followed the Arab Spring. Many countries entered a period of intense political and economic instability. The rebellion in Syria turned into a protracted and intense civil war that has widened into a complex regional conflict; extreme violence in Iraq intensified and mutated into another civil war; and Libya's and the Republic of Yemen's transitions were derailed as fighting in their territories escalated and chaos ensued with devastating consequences for civilians. Terror activity surged throughout the region as extremist networks challenged the government's monopoly over violence.

The consequences of these events for development in the MENA region have been grave, erasing decades of progress. The civil wars in Iraq, Libya, Syria, and the Republic of Yemen pushed millions of people back into poverty and dependence on humanitarian assistance. Child and maternal mortality skyrocketed, and life expectancy slumped as hundreds of thousands of people died either directly from violence or indirectly from hunger, neglect, and lack of access to health services. The wars forced millions of children out of school because many schools were destroyed, closed their doors, or were turned into shelters for the internally displaced. Economic growth collapsed in war-torn countries and slowed down substantially elsewhere in developing MENA. Inflation soared in many countries, investment plummeted, and the states' ability to finance public services was eroded as governments increased spending on national security at the expense of productive investments in public services and infrastructure. In short, the economic performance of the developing MENA region deteriorated significantly during the

FIGURE O.9

Reversal of Fortunes in Developing MENA

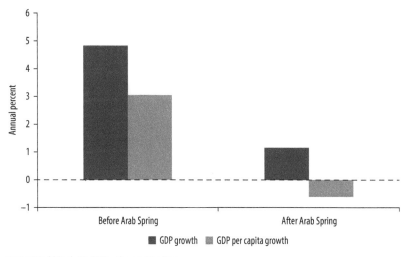

Source: World Bank, World Development Indicators.
Note: GDP = gross domestic product; MENA = Middle East and North Africa. "Before Arab Spring" covers the period from 2005 to 2010; "After Arab Spring" covers the period from 2011 to 2014.

aftermath of the Arab Spring. Annual economic growth decreased by more than half, on average, in real terms and dropped to nearly zero in per capita terms (figure O.9).

What issues contributed to the collapse of some Arab states in the post–Arab Spring period? This study identifies three important factors that distinguish the countries that managed to stay peaceful from those that plunged into conflict: (1) the quality of governance institutions for security, (2) the ability to use redistribution to appease angry populations, and (3) the intensity and type of external interventions in the context of past policies of exclusion and overlapping polarization along regional, ethnic, and sectarian lines.

Consistent with the old Arab social contract, which traded financial rewards for political support and punished dissent using sanction and deterrence institutions, this study shows that all Arab states relied on a two-pronged security model of governance to maintain political stability. Because the redistributive prong of the security model (that is, the social contract) was malfunctioning, the regimes had to rely mostly on the deterrence and sanctions mechanisms (the military, the police, and the judiciary) to stay in power and quell the surge in political violence.[8] The quality of deterrence and sanctions institutions was lowest in the four Arab countries where the uprisings turned into civil wars or conflict reemerged following a period of relative calm (figure O.10).

FIGURE O.10

Institutional Quality in Arab Economies, 2010

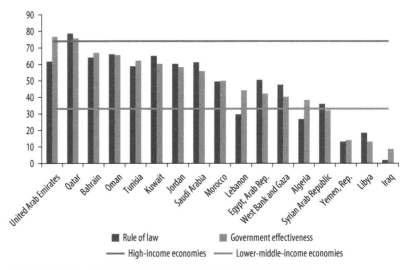

Source: World Governance Indicators Database (Kaufmann, Kraay, and Mastruzzi 2010).

Elsewhere in the region institutional quality was considerably better, signaling lower risk of political violence.

In addition, financial transfers from the Gulf states enabled an effective redistributive policy response in many of these countries. In Jordan and Morocco, monarchs not only used financial transfers from the Gulf Cooperation Council states to appease popular anger but also quickly enacted reforms that appeared to strengthen power-sharing and dispute-settlement mechanisms. In Tunisia, high institutional quality, along with low tolerance for violence and a relatively homogeneous population, reduced the risk of political violence. While the electorate was polarized between secular and Islamic visions for political and social development, political parties maintained some degree of flexibility in their positions (Lynch 2016). In Egypt, where violence surfaced sporadically during mass demonstrations, it did not have the opportunity to escalate because of the key role played by the strong military and external support for peaceful transition (Lynch 2016).

In the cases of Libya, Syria, and the Republic of Yemen, however, external interventions aimed to topple long-standing authoritarian governments.[9] According to Lynch (2016), many of these interventions were mostly uncoordinated, creating conditions for competitive arming of rebel factions and increasing the intensity of conflict. As shown in Abu Bader and Ianchovichina (2017), nonhumanitarian and nonneutral external military interventions tend to exacerbate religious polarization in the region and therefore increase the risk of high-intensity conflicts. External interventions of this type worsen the intensity of conflict because fighters who are externally supported are less likely to protect the local population since they rely less on local support.[10] In highly polarized societies, the presence of natural resources creates incentives for violence (Collier and Hoeffler 2004), while the large stock of unemployed young men lowers the costs of recruitment.

Conditions for stoking polarization along spatial, ethnic, and religious lines existed in many MENA countries before the Arab Spring. Regional and rural-urban inequalities were most substantial in Egypt, Iraq, Tunisia, and the Republic of Yemen, and were growing in Syria because of a drought that forced many farmers to migrate to urban areas. The overlap of spatial segmentation and ethnic-sectarian polarization created not only conditions for hatred across ethnic-sectarian lines, as discussed in Alesina, Michalopoulos, and Papaioannou (2016), but also opportunities for external interventions that helped turn the insurgencies in some MENA countries into large-scale civil wars. Thus, the spread of extreme violence in post–Arab Spring MENA can be traced to a combination of factors, including weak law-and-order institutions for security, limited ability to use redistributive policies, lack of inclusion, and external interventions that exacerbated the overlapping polarization along regional, ethnic, and sectarian lines, worsening the intensity of the civil conflicts.

The reliance on a fractured two-pronged governance model for security has had disastrous consequences for the region. The social contract has been an integral part of this model, offering redistributive benefits in exchange for limited voice and maintaining internal stability through coercion. Thus, the breakdown of the social contract implies a breakdown in the governance model for security, while the penal system has hardened the resolve of young activists and has made them more prone to using violence as opportunities for civil disobedience mushroomed in the post–Arab Spring period. The increased incidence of terrorism activities in the MENA region since 2011 (Kiendrebeogo and Ianchovichina 2016) is perhaps an indication that extreme measures often have extreme consequences.

In the future, there are many reasons for developing a more balanced approach to governance for security along with a new social contract. The new social contract must have at its core a strong private sector, supported by an efficient government that regulates enterprises evenhandedly and is accountable to all citizens for quality services. Governments in oil-rich countries will have to improve the efficiency of institutions managing oil wealth and invest oil rents efficiently and equitably into physical capital and intangible assets, such as institutional arrangements and skills. As pointed out by Gill et al. (2014), policies for inclusive economic growth appear to work only when they are supported by efforts to diversify economies' asset portfolios across the main types of assets: natural resources, physical capital, and intangible capital. The need for rebalancing asset portfolios has gained urgency since 2014, when oil prices plunged. After decades of state dominance, citizens must be empowered to become active participants in the private economy. To empower private entrepreneurship, governments must demonstrate their commitment to business-friendly reforms that lower the costs of doing business, reduce complex regulations protecting the rents of connected firms, and ensure unbiased application of the laws; they must also make investments that complement and do not crowd out private investment.

Building inclusive institutions will be crucial for the success of the new social contract, and it will pay off in stability, economic growth, and shared prosperity. According to Wallis (2011, 48), "impersonality—treating everyone the same without regard to their individual identity—ranks near the top of good institutional outcomes in the pantheon of growth theory." Therefore, the new governance model for security will have to be based on a balanced mix of inclusive institutions that create incentives for cooperation, fair dispute settlement, redistributive policies targeted to the most vulnerable segments of society, and rule-of-law institutions that protect and respect the rights of all citizens.

Notes

1. For details, see Gause 2011; Goodwin 2011; Bellin 2012; and Bromley 2014.
2. Gause (2011) argues that most observers, including political scientists, were unaware of the fragility of Arab autocracies, while some considered Islam a stabilizing force (Bromley 2014).
3. See, for instance, discussions of this issue in Chekir and Diwan 2012; Bromley 2014; Cammett and Diwan 2013.
4. Comparisons to household expenditures using data from the national accounts may result in issues given the large gap between micro and macro household expenditure data for Egypt. Verme et al. (2014) find that, between 2000 and 2009, Egyptian household consumption grew by about 8 percent according to national accounts data, but declined by about 8 percent according to household survey data. The gap between household income from the household surveys and that from the national accounts was larger and estimated to be 37 percent.
5. The unhappy development paradox is linked to the Easterlin (1974) paradox of growth without a corresponding increase in reported happiness levels and to Graham and Lora's (2009) "unhappy growth" paradox.
6. The Arab Spring countries—Egypt, Libya, Syria, Tunisia, and the Republic of Yemen—are the developing Arab countries with the most intense uprisings during this period.

7. The fact that violence was used to repress dissent during the time when the social contracts were supposedly working well, for example, in the Republic of Yemen (1962–70), Egypt (1977), and Syria (1980–82), suggests that exclusion in all its dimensions generated anger about relative deprivation.

8. This argument is consistent with Murshed (2009), who argues that violent conflict is essentially a manifestation of the breakdown of the social contract.

9. In Libya, a multistate NATO-led coalition launched a military intervention on March 19, 2011; the intervention aimed to protect civilian lives from attacks by government forces and later extended support to rebels who ultimately toppled the regime of Muammar Gaddafi. In the Republic of Yemen, the Gulf Cooperation Council countries backed a transitional plan for the country, which removed the president of the country, Ali Abdullah Saleh, and replaced him with his deputy, Abdrabu Mansur Hadi. In Syria, foreign involvement refers to political, military, and operational support to parties involved in the conflict. The government has received military and political support from the Russian Federation, the Islamic Republic of Iran, the Lebanese Hezbollah party, and other groups. The Syrian opposition has received financial, logistical, political, and some military support from major Sunni states in the Middle East allied with the United States. The Kurdish forces in Syria have received military and logistical support from Iraqi Kurdistan and air support from the United States, Canada, Great Britain, and France. Other groups fighting on Syrian territory have received support from Turkey and nongovernmental organizations from across the Muslim world.

10. Abu Bader and Ianchovichina (2017) find that neutral and humanitarian external military interventions are not associated with conflict incidence.

References

Abu Bader, S., and E. Ianchovichina. 2017. "Polarization, Foreign Military Interventions, and Civil Conflicts." Policy Research Working Paper 8248, World Bank, Washington, DC.

Alesina, A., S. Michalopoulos, and E. Papaioannou. 2016. "Ethnic Inequality." *Journal of Political Economy* 124 (2): 428–88.

Arampatzi, E., M. Burger, E. Ianchovichina, T. Röhricht, and R. Veenhoven. 2015. "Unhappy Development: Dissatisfaction with Life on the Eve of the Arab Spring." Policy Research Working Paper 7488, World Bank, Washington, DC.

Assaad, R., and F. Roudi-Fahimi. 2007. "Youth in the Middle East and North Africa: Demographic Opportunity or Challenge?" MENA Policy Briefs, Population Reference Bureau, Washington, DC.

Assaad, R., C. Krafft, D. Salehi-Isfahani, and J. Roemer. 2016. "Inequality of Opportunity in Income and Consumption in the Middle East and North Africa in Comparative Perspective." Working Paper 1003, Economic Research Forum, Giza, Egypt.

Atkinson, A., T. Piketty, and E. Saez. 2011. "Top Incomes in the Long Run of History." *Journal of Economic Literature* 49 (1): 3–71.

Behzadan, N., R. Chisik, H. Onder, and B. Battaile. 2017. "Does Inequality Drive the Dutch Disease? Theory and Evidence." *Journal of International Economics* 106: 103–18.

Bellin, E. 2012. "Reconsidering the Robustness of Authoritarianism in the Middle East: Lessons from the Arab Spring." *Comparative Politics* 44: 127–49.

Bromley, R. 2014. "The 'Arab Spring' Stress Test: Diagnosing Reasons for the Revolt." Working Paper, University of Wisconsin-Madison.

Burger, M., E. Ianchovichina, and B. Rijkers. 2016. "Risky Business: Political Instability and Sectoral Greenfield Foreign Direct Investment in the Arab World." *World Bank Economic Review* 30 (2): 306–31.

Cammett, M. C., and I. Diwan. 2013. *The Political Economy of the Arab Uprisings.* New York: Perseus Books Group.

Chekir, H., and I. Diwan. 2012. "Distressed Whales on the Nile—Egypt Capitalists in the Wake of the 2010 Revolution." Working Paper 250, Harvard University, Center for International Development, Cambridge, MA.

Collier, P., and A. Hoeffler. 2004. "Greed and Grievance in Civil War." *Oxford Economic Papers* 56 (4): 563–95.

Dang, H., and E. Ianchovichina. 2016. "Welfare Dynamics with Synthetic Panels: The Case of the Arab World in Transition." Policy Research Working Paper 7595, World Bank, Washington, DC.

Devarajan, S., and E. Ianchovichina. 2017. "A Broken Social Contract, Not High Inequality, Led to the Arab Spring." *Review of Income and Wealth*, published online.

Easterlin, R. A. 1974. "Does Economic Growth Improve the Human Lot? Some Empirical Evidence." In *Nations and Households in Economic Growth*, edited by P. A. David and M. W. Reder, 89–125. New York: Academic Press.

Freund, C., and M. Jaud. 2015. *Champions Wanted: Promoting Exports in the Middle East and North Africa.* Washington, DC: World Bank.

Gause III, G. F. 2011. "Why Middle East Studies Missed the Arab Spring." *Foreign Affairs* 90: 81–90.

Gill, I., I. Izvorski, W. van Eeghen, and D. de Rosa. 2014. *Diversified Development: Making the Most of Natural Resources in Eurasia.* Washington, DC: World Bank.

Goodwin, J. 2011. "Why We Were Surprised (Again) by the Arab Spring." *Swiss Political Science Review* 17: 452–56.

Graham, C., and E. Lora. 2009. "Happiness and Health Satisfaction across Countries." In *Paradox and Perception: Measuring Quality of Life in Latin America*, edited by C. Graham and E. Lora. Washington, DC: Brookings Institution Press.

Gurr, T. R. 1970. *Why Men Rebel.* Princeton, NJ: Princeton University Press.

Hassine, N. 2012. "Inequality of Opportunity in Egypt." *World Bank Economic Review* 26 (2): 265–95.

———. 2014. "Economic Inequality in the Arab Region." *World Development* 66: 532–56.

Hirschman, A., and M. Rothschild. 1973. "The Changing Tolerance for Income Inequality in the Course of Economic Development." *Quarterly Journal of Economics* 87 (4): 544–66.

Hlasny, V., and P. Verme. 2016. "Top Incomes and the Measurement of Inequality in Egypt." *World Bank Economic Review*, published online.

Hoekman, B., and K. Sekkat. 2009. "Deeper Integration of Goods, Services, Capital and Labor Markets: A Policy Research Agenda for the MENA Region." ERF Policy Research Report 32, Economic Research Forum, Giza, Egypt.

Ianchovichina, E., S. Devarajan, and M. Burger. 2013. "MENA Economic and Development Prospects 2013: Investing in Turbulent Times." Other Operational Studies 20562, World Bank, Washington, DC.

Iqbal, F., and Y. Kiendrebeogo. 2016. "The Determinants of Child Mortality Reduction in the Middle East and North Africa." *Middle East Development Journal* 8: (2).

Johannesen, N. 2015. "Economic Inequality in the MENA Countries—Evidence from Cross-Border Deposits." Unpublished.

Kaufmann, D., A. Kraay, and M. Mastruzzi. 2010. "The Worldwide Governance Indicators: Methodology and Analytical Issues." Policy Research Working Paper 5430, World Bank, Washington, DC.

Kiendrebeogo, Y., and E. Ianchovichina. 2016. "Who Supports Violent Extremism in Developing Countries? Analysis of Attitudes Based on Value Surveys." Policy Research Working Paper 7691, World Bank, Washington, DC.

Lakner, C., and B. Milanovic. 2013. "Global Income Distribution: From the Fall of the Berlin Wall to the Great Recession." *World Bank Economic Review* 30 (2): 203–32.

Lynch, M. 2016. *The New Arab Wars: Uprisings and Anarchy in the Middle East.* New York: Public Affairs.

Muller, E. 1985. "Income Inequality, Regime Repressiveness, and Political Violence." *American Sociological Review* 50: 47–67.

Murshed, M. 2009. "Conflict as the Absence of Contract." *Economics of Peace and Security Journal* 4 (1): 32–38.

Ncube, M., and J. Anyanwu. 2012. "Inequality and Arab Spring Revolutions in North Africa and the Middle East." *Africa Economic Brief* 3 (7), African Development Bank, Abidjan, Côte d'Ivoire.

Nimeh, Z. 2012. "Economic Growth and Inequality in the Middle East: An Explanation of the Arab Spring?" ISPI Analysis No. 105, April, Istituto per Gli Studi di Politica Internazionale, Milan.

Osborn, B. 2011. "The Arab Spring, As Seen from 2014: A Fight for Prosperity, Not Power." Global Envision. http://www.globalenvision.org/2011/12/19/arab-spring-seen-2015-fight-prosperity-not-power.

Ostry, J., A. Berg, and C. Tsangarides. 2014. "Redistribution, Inequality, and Growth." IMF Staff Discussion Note, International Monetary Fund, Washington, DC.

Rijkers, B., C. Freund, and A. Nucifora. 2017. "All in the Family: State Capture in Tunisia." *Journal of Development Economics* 124 (C): 41–59.

Schiffbauer, M., A. Sy, S. Hussain, H. Sahnoun, and P. Keefer. 2015. *Jobs or Privileges: Unleashing the Employment Potential of the Middle East and North Africa.* MENA Development Report. Washington, DC: World Bank.

van der Weide, R., C. Lakner, and E. Ianchovichina. Forthcoming. "Is Inequality Underestimated in Egypt? Evidence from House Prices." *Review of Income and Wealth*, accepted for publication.

Verme, P., B. Milanovic, S. Al-Shawarby, S. El-Tawila, M. Gadallah, and
    E. El-Majeed. 2014. *Inside Inequality in the Arab Republic of Egypt: Facts and
    Perceptions across People, Time, and Space.* Washington, DC: World Bank.
Wallis, J. 2011. "Institutions, Organizations, Impersonality, and Interests:
    The Dynamics of Institutions." *Journal of Economic Behavior and Organization*
    79: 48–64.

PART 1

The "Arab Inequality" Puzzle

The Arab Spring uprisings brought issues of equity and inclusion to the forefront of public attention. The Arab Republic of Egypt, in particular, generated considerable interest because income inequality was cited as one of the factors behind the Egyptian revolution (Hlasny and Verme 2016; Nimeh 2012; Ncube and Anyanwu 2012; Osborn 2011). The idea that income inequality is linked to political upheaval is not new and can be traced to ancient times when social philosophers speculated that economic inequality is a fundamental cause of civil unrest (Muller 1985). Today, high income inequality is recognized to be bad for social consensus and political stability, which, in turn, could harm investment, sustainable growth, and progress in human development (Ostry, Berg, and Tsangarides 2014). In addition, tolerance for income inequality varies over time and across countries (Hirschman and Rothschild 1973).

Yet, the idea that income inequality was a major factor in the revolts poses a puzzle. This so-called Arab inequality puzzle arises because protests occurred in countries that appear to be among some of the most equal countries in the world. The World Bank's PovcalNet, a database of household income and consumption surveys from around the globe, is one of the best sources of data on inequality across countries and time periods. The Gini coefficient is arguably the most commonly used measure of inequality; it ranges between 0 and 1, with values closer to 0 indicating lower inequality. According to these data, available for 135 countries around the period 2008–09, the Gini coefficients for the countries in the Middle East and North Africa region were neither rising nor high by international standards (figure P1.1).

This part of the book first explores economic inequality trends in Arab states during the decades preceding the Arab Spring and, to the extent possible, uses new data and techniques to more accurately assess the extent of inequality in Arab states. It then turns to distributional concerns

FIGURE P1.1

Inequality, over Time and across the World

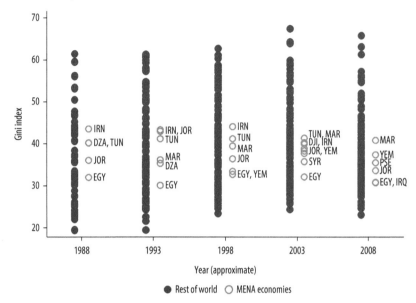

Source: Data from Lakner and Milanovic 2013.
Note: MENA = Middle East and North Africa. DJI = Djibouti; DZA = Algeria; EGY = Arab Republic of Egypt; IRN = Islamic Republic of Iran; IRQ = Iraq; JOR = Jordan; MAR = Morocco; PSE = West Bank and Gaza; SYR = Syrian Arab Republic; YEM = The Republic of Yemen.

related to poverty and intragenerational welfare mobility. The question of whether popular anger has been rising in response to rising economic inequality or a middle-class squeeze is an important one; depending on the answer, different remedies would be appropriate.

References

Hirschman, A., and M. Rothschild. 1973. "The Changing Tolerance for Income Inequality in the Course of Economic Development." *Quarterly Journal of Economics* 87 (4): 544–66.

Hlasny, V., and P. Verme. 2016. "Top Incomes and the Measurement of Inequality in Egypt." *World Bank Economic Review*, published online.

Lakner, C., and B. Milanovic. 2013. "Global Income Distribution: From the Fall of the Berlin Wall to the Great Recession." *World Bank Economic Review* 30 (2): 203–32.

Milanovic, B. 2014. "Description of ALL THE GINIS Database." World Bank, Washington, DC.

Muller, E. 1985. "Income Inequality, Regime Repressiveness, and Political Violence." *American Sociological Review* 50: 47–67.

Ncube, M., and J. Anyanwu. 2012. "Inequality and Arab Spring Revolutions in North Africa and the Middle East." *Africa Economic Brief* 3 (7), African Development Bank, Abidjan, Côte d'Ivoire.

Nimeh, Z. 2012. "Economic Growth and Inequality in the Middle East: An Explanation of the Arab Spring?" ISPI Analysis No. 105, April, Istituto per Gli Studi di Politica Internazionale, Milan.

Osborn, B. 2011. "The Arab Spring, As Seen from 2014: A Fight for Prosperity, Not Power." *Global Envision* blog. http://www.globalenvision.org/2011/12/19/arab-spring-seen-2015-fight-prosperity-not-power.

Ostry, J., A. Berg, and C. Tsangarides. 2014. "Redistribution, Inequality, and Growth." IMF Staff Discussion Note, International Monetary Fund, Washington, DC.

CHAPTER 1

Economic Inequality: Measurement and Biases

Introduction

Measuring economic inequality accurately is a difficult task, particularly in developing countries where comprehensive administrative information on income and wealth is generally unavailable. Inequality measures are often biased because they are based on household surveys that suffer from several well-known shortcomings. Apart from the difficulty of recalling income and wealth information correctly, survey respondents may under-report expenditures or deliberately leave out income and wealth that result from illegal or informal activities. In addition, these surveys typically include few individuals at the very top of the income distribution, even though accurately capturing the "top 1 percent" is crucial to estimating inequality (Alvaredo 2011). In the Middle East and North Africa (MENA), these difficulties are compounded because access to household surveys has been limited. Thus, it is not surprising that there is confusion on the topic. To date few studies have focused on economic inequality in Arab countries. Lack of access to and comparability of household surveys has constrained cross-country analysis of expenditure inequality in the region.

This report relies on a set of harmonized household surveys conducted during different years in different countries before 2010 to develop an understanding of issues linked to economic inequality and, in subsequent chapters, to economic mobility. The data set, discussed in detail in Hassine (2014) and presented in table 1.1, contains a set of household surveys for six Arab economies: the Arab Republic of Egypt, Jordan, the Syrian Arab Republic, Tunisia, the West Bank and Gaza, and the Republic of Yemen. These household surveys have been harmonized for comparability both across countries and within countries over time using

TABLE 1.1

Survey Years and Poverty Rates at $2/day in 2005 PPP$

Country/economy	Survey name	Survey years	Poverty rate (percent) First period	Second period
Egypt, Arab Rep.	Household Income, Expenditure and Consumption Survey	2004, 2009	19.0	28.6
Jordan	Household Expenditure and Income Survey	2006, 2008	3.8	2.2
Syrian Arab Rep.	Household Budget Survey	1997, 2004	38.8	7.5
Tunisia	Household Budget Consumption and Living Standards Survey	2005, 2010	8.0	4.6
West Bank and Gaza	Palestine Expenditure and Consumption Survey	2005, 2009	1.5	0.7
Yemen, Rep.	Household Budget Survey	1998, 2006	31.7	54.5
Average			17.1	16.4

Source: Dang and Ianchovichina 2016, using household survey expenditure data.
Note: PPP$ = purchasing-power-parity dollars.

methodologies developed by the World Bank, the Luxemburg Income Study, the Organisation for Economic Co-operation and Development, and country statistical offices, as described in Hassine (2014). All expenditure data used in this analysis have been deflated by the consumer price index of the respective economy and year, and adjustments for spatial price differences have been made for Egypt, Syria, and the West Bank and Gaza.[1] The purchasing-power-parity (PPP) conversion factor for private consumption (local currency unit per international dollar), obtained from the World Bank's World Development Indicators database, is used to facilitate comparison of consumption expenditure levels across economies. Only for the West Bank and Gaza is the PPP conversion factor for gross domestic product (GDP) used instead.

Because assessments of economic inequality should ideally reflect wealth disparities, the study also exploits the *Forbes* database of billionaires and a data set from the Bank for International Settlements (BIS) on cross-border bank deposits of nationals from various countries around the world into 43 countries, representing all major financial centers including tax havens.

Income Inequality

In a study of the MENA region, Hassine (2014) presents a comprehensive, in-depth comparison of expenditure inequality across 11 economies,[2] using harmonized microdata from 26 household surveys and three different consumption expenditure aggregates. The investigation—which takes into account temporal and, in some cases, within-country variations in the cost of living—confirms the low to moderate levels of expenditure inequality in the region (figure 1.1). However, it argues that the coverage

FIGURE 1.1

The Arab Region's Development Context

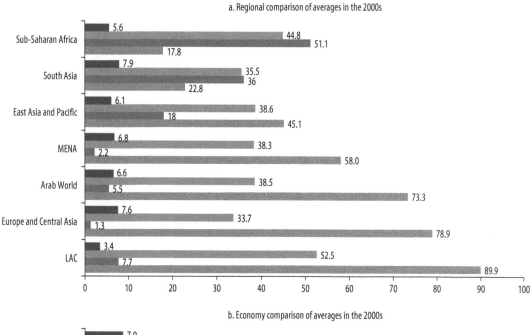

a. Regional comparison of averages in the 2000s

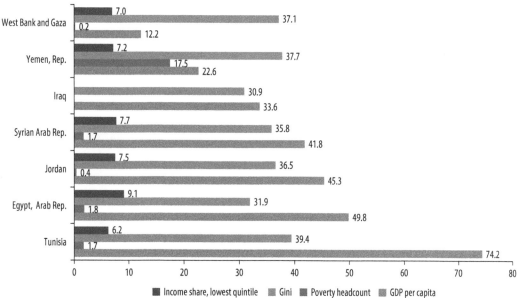

b. Economy comparison of averages in the 2000s

■ Income share, lowest quintile ■ Gini ■ Poverty headcount ■ GDP per capita

Source: Hassine 2014, using World Bank World Development Indicators (2013) and PovcalNet databases.
Note: Gross domestic product (GDP) is in hundreds of 2005 purchasing-power-parity international dollars. Poverty headcount calculated using $1.25/person/day in 2005 PPP$. Gini coefficient presented as a percentage. LAC = Latin America and the Caribbean; MENA = Middle East and North Africa.

of items in households' expenditures has a significant effect on the Gini measures of inequality. The Gini index, based on food and nonfood expenditures and represented in percentages, is, on average, 4.2 points higher than the Gini based on food alone; including expenditures on durables and housing increases the Gini by about 0.5 point.

A diverse picture of within-country expenditure inequality and its evolution emerges from the analysis in Hassine (2014). Inequality was low in Libya and Egypt and moderate in the rest of the Arab economies for which information was available (figure 1.2). There is no discernible pattern in the evolution of inequality through time and relative to average welfare. Over time, total expenditure inequality declined in Egypt, Jordan, and Tunisia, and increased in Djibouti, Syria, the West Bank and Gaza, and the Republic of Yemen (figure 1.2); but even then the Gini index remained moderate, averaging 38.5 for the region as a whole.

Expenditure inequality appears to have no relationship to average per capita expenditures or welfare. Both expenditure inequality and average per capita expenditure increased in Syria and the West Bank and Gaza and decreased in Egypt, while welfare improved with a decline in inequality in Jordan and Tunisia. The opposite was observed in the Republic of Yemen and Djibouti (figure 1.2), where the low income and high inequality

FIGURE 1.2

Comparisons of Expenditure Inequality in Developing MENA

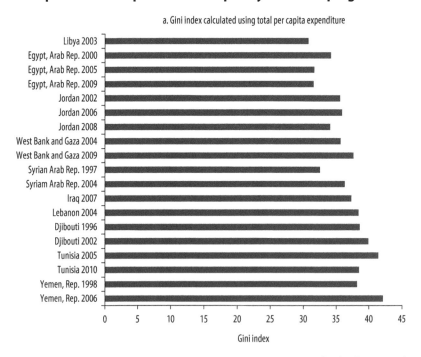

a. Gini index calculated using total per capita expenditure

(continued on next page)

FIGURE 1.2

Comparisons of Expenditure Inequality in Developing
MENA *Continued*

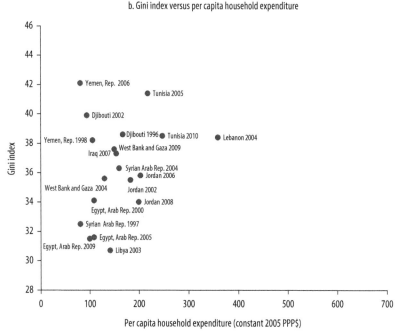

b. Gini index versus per capita household expenditure

Source: Hassine 2014.
Note: Total expenditure per capita includes expenditure on food, nonfood, housing, and durables. Gini coefficient presented as a percentage. PPP int. $ = purchasing-power-parity international dollars.

pattern deepened. Growth was more broadly shared in Jordan and Tunisia, but not in Syria and the West Bank and Gaza; expenditures contracted in real terms in Egypt, but most of the burden fell on top earners.

Relying on expenditure data from household surveys to gauge the extent of economic inequality and shared prosperity, however, has well-known pitfalls. Expenditure inequality may be understated because of the tendency for the top tail of the distribution to be underrepresented (Atkinson, Piketty, and Saez 2011). For this reason, analysts use administrative data, typically tax records, to estimate the income of the very rich, and thereby obtain a more accurate description of the "true" income distribution. However, the availability of tax record data, particularly in MENA countries, is still limited (Alvaredo and Piketty 2014). The World Top Incomes Database (Alvaredo et al. 2015) includes no MENA countries. Furthermore, data derived from tax records become less useful as tax evasion becomes more pervasive, which is particularly important in developing countries, including some Arab economies.

In the absence of tax data and in search of evidence of a higher level of expenditure inequality in Egypt, Hlasny and Verme (2016) adjust the upper tail of the distribution using the Pareto distribution, often used to describe the allocation of wealth and income in a society.[3] They find that expenditure inequality in Egypt does not increase substantially, possibly because their Pareto distribution is fitted using the household survey, which underestimates the top tail.

Van der Weide, Lakner, and Ianchovichina (forthcoming) get around this problem by estimating the upper tail of the distribution using market house price data from large metropolitan areas in urban Egypt.[4] The advantages of this approach are that market house price data are publicly available and relatively easy to obtain using technology; there is no systematic tendency for the data to understate home values, in contrast to income data, which may be underreported on tax returns; and the top end of the distribution is well captured in these data because market price information is applicable to homes owned by the top tail. Van der Weide, Lakner, and Ianchovichina (forthcoming) then combine the top tail of the imputed consumption distribution with the bottom of the expenditure distribution obtained from the household survey.[5] They find that the Gini index based on expenditure data for urban Egypt increases to 47 after corrections for missing top incomes from 36 when using only the household survey (table 1.2). As expected, income inequality is greater than expenditure inequality, with the Gini index based on income data for urban Egypt reaching 51.8 after correcting for the missing top tail from 38.5 when using only the household survey data (table 1.2). The mean log deviation measure and the Theil index similarly adjust upward, as expected. The results provide evidence that the level of inequality in urban Egypt has been significantly underestimated. The results are consistent with perception data that

TABLE 1.2

Estimates of Consumption and Income Inequality Indexes for Urban Egypt, Fiscal Year 2008/09

	Survey and house prices	Survey only
Consumption inequality		
Gini	47.0	36.4
Mean log deviation	27.8	21.7
Theil	42.0	25.8
Income inequality		
Gini	51.8	38.5
Mean log deviation	37.4	24.4
Theil	73.8	30.2

Source: van der Weide, Lakner, and Ianchovichina, forthcoming.

FIGURE 1.3

Inequality in Subjective Well-Being, 2006–09

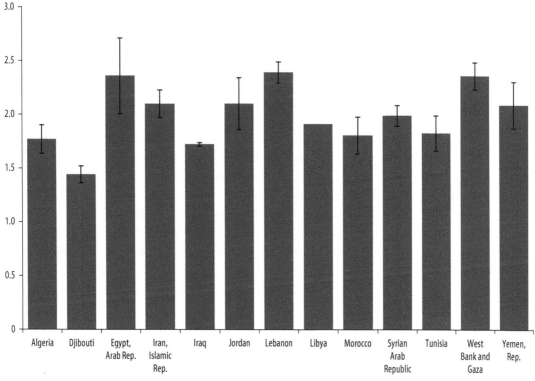

Source: Gallup World Poll.
Note: Figure shows inequality in average life evaluation measured as standard deviation in life evaluation, shown along with 95 percent confidence intervals.

show that, before the Arab Spring, inequality in subjective well-being in Egypt was much higher than in most other MENA economies and was comparable to that in Lebanon (figure 1.3).

However, the declining trend in expenditure inequality in Tunisia and Egypt, where the Arab Spring uprisings first took place, has been pronounced, as suggested by Verme et al. (2014) and Hassine (2012, 2014). Furthermore, inequality of opportunity—an undesirable type of inequality associated with circumstances beyond an individual's control—is also found to be low in a number of Arab countries in the years preceding the Arab Spring events (Hassine 2012; Assaad et al. 2016).

Wealth Inequality

An investigation of monetary inequality would be incomplete without a discussion of wealth disparity. Thus, this section examines various measures of wealth inequality, which is typically much higher and more socially divisive but harder to detect than expenditure or income inequality. Measuring wealth is more complex than calculating income because data on wealth are scarce, especially in developing MENA. To get a glimpse of the concentration of wealth at the top of the income ladder, different sources of information must be combined; although each source may not be perfect, together they provide a picture of wealth inequality.

One way to assess the degree of wealth concentration in MENA countries and compare it with that of other countries is to use *Forbes'* data on the net worth of billionaires.[6] According to these data, wealth concentration in MENA countries is less than wealth concentration in other countries at similar levels of development (figure 1.4).[7] To be sure, these data reflect mostly wealth in publicly traded companies, and very few companies in the region are publicly traded (OECD 2009). The 20 or so largest companies in most Gulf states, Egypt, Lebanon, and Morocco are not listed on national or world stock exchanges. Instead, they are either firms

FIGURE 1.4

Wealth Concentrated in the Hands of Billionaires

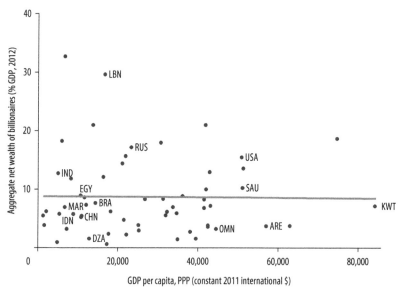

Source: Ianchovichina, Mottaghi, and Devarajan 2015, based on *Forbes* database of billionaires and World Bank data on GDP.
Note: GDP = gross domestic product; PPP = purchasing power parity. The solid line in the figure is the linear trend line. BRA = Brazil; CHN = China; DZA = Algeria; EGY = Arab Republic of Egypt; IDN = Indonesia; IND = India; KWT = Kuwait; LBN = Lebanon; MAR = Morocco; OMN = Oman; RUS = Russian Federation; SAU = Saudi Arabia; ARE = United Arab Emirates; USA = United States.

privately owned by prominent families or state-owned firms. This situation makes it hard to identify and track the wealth of the region's billionaires, and it also suggests that ordinary people cannot share in the prosperity generated by the most successful firms in the Arab countries.

Another way to gauge the extent of wealth inequality is to estimate the size of wealth hidden in tax haven bank deposits, available from the BIS in a data set on cross-border bank deposits.[8] The focus on bank deposits in tax havens is warranted for at least a couple of reasons. First, haven deposits offer advantages to individuals wishing to hide their wealth, notably banking secrecy and legal arrangements that nominally sever the tie between the assets and their owners. Such arrangements are likely to be most appealing to individuals who want to hide their wealth status because the wealth may have been acquired through informal or illegal means. Second, accounts in foreign banks typically involve fixed costs that are prohibitive for individuals at lower wealth levels. The data on bank deposits in tax havens therefore offer insights about the hidden wealth of the wealthiest who are underrepresented in household surveys, even when these surveys have been corrected for missing observations at the top end of the distribution.

However, this data set has important limitations. It covers only bank deposits and excludes other types of hidden wealth such as bonds or equity owned through haven accounts. Zucman (2013) estimates that bank deposits account for roughly one-quarter of the financial wealth of the world's wealthiest individuals. The data set does not distinguish between deposits belonging to individuals, firms, and governments, and assigns deposits to counterpart countries on the basis of immediate rather than ultimate ownership. Thus, if a resident of Tunisia owns a corporation in Panama, which in turn holds a bank account in Switzerland, the BIS statistics will record the Swiss account as belonging to a resident of Panama. Corporations, trusts, and other similar arrangements are frequently used by owners of hidden wealth to add layers of secrecy (Financial Action Task Force 2011). Johannesen (2015) controls for this problem by excluding deposits recorded as belonging to havens because such deposits are very likely to reflect sham structures rather than true ownership by haven residents.

Using this data set, Johannesen (2015) studies the distribution of bank deposits in tax havens across countries and over time and finds that, historically, hidden wealth has been considerably larger for MENA countries than elsewhere, but this difference has diminished rapidly in recent years (figure 1.5). Furthermore, he finds no correlation between the shares of haven deposits in GDP and the level of expenditure inequality in MENA (table 1.3).

FIGURE 1.5

Offshore Bank Deposits in Tax Havens

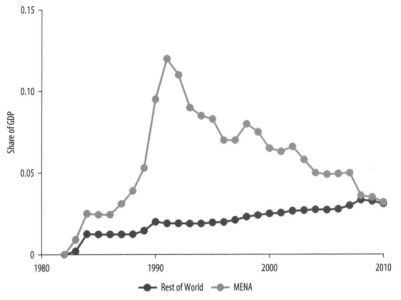

Source: Johannesen 2015.
Note: GDP = gross domestic product; MENA = Middle East and North Africa.

TABLE 1.3

Correlation between the Ratio of Haven Deposits to GDP and the Gini Coefficient

	All countries	Low income	Middle income	High income	MENA	Non-MENA
Gini coefficient	0.000297	0.000102	0.000413	0.00205*	−0.000723	0.000398*
	(0.000283)	(0.000417)	(0.000414)	(0.00106)	(0.00674)	(0.00024)
Constant	0.0115	0.0153	0.00617	−0.035	0.0721	0.00584
	(0.0113)	(0.0165)	(0.0172)	(0.0351)	(0.236)	(0.00959)
Observations	113	38	58	18	7	106
R^2	0.010	0.002	0.017	0.189	0.002	0.026

Source: Johannesen 2015.
Note: GDP = gross domestic product; MENA = Middle East and North Africa. The dependent variable is the ratio of haven deposits to GDP. The value of the Gini coefficient is between 0 and 1. Standard errors are shown in parentheses.
* significant at the 10 percent level.

In sum, although existing measures of inequality may underestimate its true level, according to these measures the extent of economic inequality was moderate by international standards, and the undesirable inequality of opportunity was low in many MENA countries. An important note is that in Tunisia and Egypt, where the Arab Spring uprisings happened first, income inequality declined before the Arab Spring, and the gap between MENA and the rest of the world in wealth in offshore haven bank deposits disappeared by 2010. These empirical findings are consistent with a profile of economies that rely on redistributive policies.[9] The post-independence, state-led economic model adopted by these countries contributed to poverty reduction and equity over the years, including during the past two decades, but relied on redistributive fiscal policies that became unsustainable over time (Devarajan and Mottaghi 2015). Fiscal imbalances grew, reflecting disappointing growth in the 1980s and increasing recurrent expenditures on public wages and food and energy subsidies. Substantial increases in international commodity prices in the 2000s and fast-growing domestic demand increased the fiscal cost of subsidies and provided impetus for initiating reforms to the subsidy programs (Devarajan et al. 2014). Most governments, however, continued to offer food and energy subsidies, given that reforms were often partial or reversed under public pressure (for example, World Bank 2011a, 2011b). The evidence in this chapter suggests that rising economic inequality did not trigger the Arab Spring events, although inequality measures based on monetary data clearly understate the true level of inequality visible in perception data on well-being. In search of answers to the Arab inequality puzzle, the next chapter investigates issues of economic mobility and welfare dynamics in the years before the eruptions of popular Arab anger and presents evidence of the middle-class squeeze.

Notes

1. The absence of spatial price differentials prevented adjustments for regional price differentials in Jordan, Tunisia, and the Republic of Yemen.
2. The set of economies includes Djibouti, Egypt, Iraq, Jordan, Lebanon, Libya, Syria, Tunisia, the United Arab Emirates, the West Bank and Gaza, and the Republic of Yemen.
3. The Pareto distribution shows that a large portion of the wealth of a society is owned by a small percentage of people.
4. They assembled a data set of real estate prices by extracting information from listings of homes for sale or rent, available at Egyptian websites.
5. The authors follow the method in Alvaredo (2011) and Diaz-Bazan (2014).
6. The list is regularly updated and is available at http://www.forbes.com /billionaires/list/.
7. Wealth concentration in most MENA countries would rise if the estimated wealth of current and former heads of state were included.
8. The data set contains information on foreign-owned bank deposits in 43 countries—representing all major financial centers, including tax havens—at the bilateral level.

9. Benabou (2000) argues that, with imperfect credit and insurance markets, some redistributive policies can improve ex ante welfare, and the popular support for redistribution decreases with inequality. Therefore, there might be multiple steady states: mutually reinforcing high inequality and low redistribution or low inequality and high redistribution.

References

Alvaredo, F. 2011. "A Note on the Relationship between Top Income Shares and the Gini Coefficient." *Economics Letters* 110 (3): 274–77.

Alvaredo, F., and T. Piketty. 2014. "Measuring Top Incomes and Inequality in the Middle East: Data Limitations and Illustration with the Case of Egypt." Working Paper No. 832, Economic Research Forum, Cairo, Egypt.

Alvaredo, F., A. Atkinson, T. Piketty, and E. Saez. 2015. The World Top Incomes Database. http://topincomes.g-mond.parisschoolofeconomics.eu/.

Assaad, R., C. Krafft, J. Roemer, and D. Salehi-Isfahani. 2016. "Inequality of Opportunity in Income and Consumption: The Middle East and North Africa Region in Comparative Perspective." Working Paper 1003, Economic Research Forum, Cairo, Egypt.

Atkinson, A. B., T. Piketty, and E. Saez. 2011. "Top Incomes in the Long Run of History." *Journal of Economic Literature* 49 (1): 3–71.

Benabou, R. 2000. "Unequal Societies: Income Distribution and the Social Contract." *American Economic Review* 90 (1): 96–129.

Dang, H.-A., and E. Ianchovichina. 2016. "Welfare Dynamics with Synthetic Panels: The Case of the Arab World in Transition." Policy Research Working Paper 7595, World Bank, Washington, DC.

Devarajan, S., and L. Mottaghi. 2015. "Towards a New Social Contract." *MENA Economic Monitor*, April, World Bank, Washington, DC.

Devarajan, S., L. Mottaghi, F. Iqbal, G. Mundaca, T. Laursen, M. Vagliasindi, S. Commander, and I. Chaal-Dabi. 2014. "Corrosive Subsidies." *MENA Economic Monitor*, October, World Bank, Washington, DC.

Diaz-Bazan, T. 2014. "Measuring Inequality from Top to Bottom." Policy Research Working Paper 7237, World Bank, Washington, DC.

Financial Action Task Force. 2011. *Laundering the Proceeds of Corruption*. Paris: FATF.

Hassine, N. 2012. "Inequality of Opportunity in Egypt." *World Bank Economic Review* 26 (2): 265–95.

———. 2014. "Income Inequality in the Arab Region." *World Development* 66: 532–56.

Hlasny, V., and P. Verme. 2016. "Top Incomes and the Measurement of Inequality in Egypt." *World Bank Economic Review*, published online.

Ianchovichina, E., L. Mottaghi, and S. Devarajan. 2015. "Inequality, Uprisings, and Conflict in the Arab World." *Middle East and North Africa Economic Monitor*, October, World Bank, Washington, DC.

Johannesen, N. 2015. "Economic Inequality in the MENA Countries—Evidence from Cross-Border Deposits." Unpublished, World Bank, Washington, DC.

OECD (Organisation for Economic Co-operation and Development). 2009. *Ownership Structures in MENA Countries: Listed Companies, State-Owned, Family*

Enterprises and Some Policy Implications. Paris: OECD. http://www.oecd.org /mena/investment/ 35402110.pdf.

van der Weide, R., C. Lakner, and E. Ianchovichina. Forthcoming. "Is Inequality Underestimated in Egypt? Evidence from House Prices." *Review of Income and Wealth*, accepted for publication.

Verme, P., B. Milanovic, S. Al-Shawarby, S. El Tawila, M. Gadallah, and A. El-Majeed. 2014. *Inside Inequality in the Arab Republic of Egypt: Facts and Perceptions across People, Time, and Space.* Washington, DC: World Bank.

World Bank. 2011a. *Middle East and North Africa: Facing Challenges and Opportunities.* Economic Developments and Prospects Report. Washington, DC: World Bank.

———. 2011b. *Middle East and North Africa: Investing for Growth and Jobs.* Economic Developments and Prospects Report. Washington, DC: World Bank.

Zucman, G. 2013. "The Missing Wealth of Nations: Are Europe and the U.S. Net Debtors or Net Creditors?" *Quarterly Journal of Economics* 128 (3): 1321–64.

CHAPTER 2

Welfare Dynamics: Definitions and Measurement

Introduction

Analysis of welfare dynamics, defined as movements of individuals across welfare groups over the course of a decade or less, is crucial for understanding how development affects different groups within society and how to design effective development policies. Without a clear understanding of the processes underlying class dynamics, policies may not be able to successfully address key challenges faced by different groups of people. Analyses based solely on changes in the headcount of a welfare group cannot offer any insights into the nature of mobility. For instance, a constant poverty headcount across two rounds of cross-sectional household data may mask a situation of extreme volatility in which nearly all the poor households in the first period escape poverty and are replaced by nonpoor households in the first period that fall into poverty in the second period. Alternatively, an unchanged poverty headcount may represent a situation of near stagnation in which most households see no change in their welfare and remain chronically poor. These very different situations emerge as a result of different policies and require distinctly different policy interventions to address them effectively. Whereas strong social protection programs would most effectively address transitory poverty (because they help prevent nonpoor but vulnerable households from falling into poverty), chronic poverty may only be ameliorated with longer-term investments in human capital and infrastructure.

Understanding how different income groups' welfare evolves can be useful not only for the design of policies aimed at eliminating chronic poverty and achieving shared prosperity, but also for gauging risks to political stability. Middle-class consensus, defined by Easterly (2001) as a high share of income for the middle class and a low degree of ethnic division, has been associated with economic growth, development achievements, political stability, and reduced risk of civil wars. Negative middle-class welfare dynamics may be indicative of an eroding middle-class consensus, which, in turn, may signal not only the presence of economic problems but also higher risk of political instability, especially in polarized societies.

Defining the Middle Class

Defining the middle class is not a straightforward task. Two papers discuss ideas that can help define the middle class in the context of the Middle East and North Africa (MENA) region. The first one is by Abu-Ismail and Sarangi (2013), who apply different definitions of the middle class to household data for the Arab Republic of Egypt and the MENA region as a whole.[1] They show that different definitions lead to dramatically different middle-class sizes in the Arab world and other developing regions. For instance, Abu-Ismail and Sarangi (2013) show that the estimated size of the MENA middle class is either implausibly small, less than 5 percent of the population with the definitions proposed by Ferreira et al. (2013) and Birdsall (2007), or implausibly large, accounting for more than three-quarters of the population with the definitions in Ravallion (2010) and Chun (2010). Ali (2011), who defines the middle class using the national poverty line converted to purchasing-power-parity (PPP) dollars as the lower bound and $13 per day as the upper bound, also overestimates the size of the middle class given that the vulnerable are considered part of the middle class.

In their paper, Abu-Ismail and Sarangi (2013) argue that most definitions of the middle class have problems. *Relative definitions*, which rely on thresholds based on deviations from the economy's median per capita income, mostly provide information about the middle strata in income terms in each country. However, such definitions can be inappropriate because the median income may lie below the nationally defined poverty line. *Absolute definitions* rely on fixed thresholds and PPP exchange rates, which arguably do not appropriately adjust purchasing power across countries (Deaton 2010). Absolute thresholds will have to differ across countries and time to be useful for making inferences about the size of the middle class, especially in MENA. The region comprises low-income, lower-middle-income, upper-middle-income, and high-income economies, so the income distributions of the low- and high-income countries may not even overlap. Furthermore, fixed thresholds cannot capture the differential price effects within countries and other important welfare effects that are incorporated into the estimation of national poverty lines.

For Egypt, the income distribution implied by the relative definition used by the World Bank to define the shared prosperity concept, which focuses on the bottom 40 percent of the distribution, is approximately consistent with the one implied by the absolute definition in Abu-Ismail and Sarangi (2013). They estimate lower and upper thresholds for middle-class measurement in Egypt and determine that in 2011 the lower Egyptian poverty line, also labeled the food poverty line, was equivalent to 2005 PPP$2.3 per day; the upper poverty line, which includes expenditure on food and essential nonfood items, was 2005 PPP$3 per day; and the upper threshold for middle-class measurement, which includes expenditure on nonessential food and nonfood items, was 2005 PPP$6 per day. According to this definition, in 2011, 25 percent of Egyptians were poor and lived below the lower poverty line; another 22 percent were vulnerable and lived between the lower and upper poverty lines; the next 45 percent of the population represented the middle class; and the top 7 percent were the affluent. This definition indicates that, on the eve of the Arab Spring, the bottom 40 percent of Egyptians included all of the poor and nearly all of those vulnerable to falling into poverty.

An alternative way to define income groups is to ask people if they consider themselves to be poor, middle class, or rich, as in Ferreira et al. (2013) and cross-check the outcomes with those obtained using objective definitions based on either absolute or relative threshold measures. Cross-checking is important because Ferreira et al. (2013) find that reported middle-class status was associated with people fairly high in the income distribution in Latin America and the Caribbean. Similarly, self-reported poor status might include middle-class individuals who feel vulnerable.

This study uses two approaches to defining the middle class.[2] The first one—a hybrid combination of the relative and absolute definitions of income groups—is in line with the shared prosperity definition adopted by the World Bank (Basu 2013). With this approach, the thresholds are set in the first period so that (1) the first and second quintiles of the income or expenditure distribution represent the poor and vulnerable people in a country or the bottom 40 percent; (2) the third and fourth quintiles represent the middle class or the middle 40 percent; and (3) the fifth quintile or the top 20 percent represents the elites or the affluent.[3] The income thresholds determined in the first period are then kept fixed in the second period, allowing changes in the sizes of the three income groups to be measured.

The second approach follows Dang and Lanjouw (2016b) and uses the existing national or international poverty line to define the poor category. It then further disaggregates the nonpoor group into two subcategories: a group that is currently nonpoor but facing a significant risk of falling into poverty in the next period (that is, mostly people who belong to the lower-middle-income group), and the remaining group of people who belong to the upper middle class and the affluent. This approach derives the vulnerability line from a specified vulnerability index P, defined as the percentage of the nonpoor population in the first period that falls into poverty in the second period.

In particular, given a specified vulnerability index P, the vulnerability line V_1 can be empirically obtained from the following equality $P = P (Y_2 \leq Z_2 \mid Z_1 < Y_1 < V_1)$ because there is a one-to-one mapping between P and V_1, and the latter is also decreasing in the former (Dang and Lanjouw 2016b). In other words, the vulnerability line is the highest income level among currently nonpoor people who have a specified probability of falling into poverty in the next period.[4] As in the cases of India, the United States, and Vietnam (Dang and Lanjouw 2016a, 2016b; Rama et al. 2015), the vulnerability line in this study corresponds to a 20 percent probability of falling into poverty in the next period.

These two approaches are complementary along several dimensions. The first approach applies a fixed threshold to the income distribution, whereas the second approach takes into account the dynamics of income change over time to adjust the vulnerability line. Depending on income levels and the poverty line, the bottom 40 percent of the income distribution can accommodate a variety of poverty scenarios, ranging from consisting of all the poor but excluding some of them to consisting of all the poor but also including some of the nonpoor. Thus, by explicitly focusing on the population below the poverty line rather than on the bottom 40 percent, the second approach can better track changes in the size of the poor group. Finally, because the income distribution varies by country, the fixed thresholds under the first approach are country specific; therefore, this approach is not well-suited for cross-country comparisons. The second approach, however, obtains region-wide vulnerability and middle-class thresholds and therefore can be used to make inferences at the regional level.[5]

The country-specific thresholds based on the two definitions are shown in table 2.1.[6] The numbers in the table suggest that the bottom 40 percent represent the poor and the vulnerable to different extents across countries. For example, the bottom 40 percent in Egypt includes all the poor and some of the vulnerable to poverty because the cutoff line for the 40th percentile is PPP$2.5/day, which is slightly higher than the national absolute poverty line.[7] By contrast, in Syria, the threshold of the bottom 40 percent is very close to the national absolute poverty line, implying that the low-income group primarily includes the absolutely poor people in the first survey round.

The thresholds based on the second definition are simpler and set for the whole region. They are PPP$2/day and PPP$4.9/day for the poverty and the vulnerability lines, respectively. The poverty threshold

TABLE 2.1

Thresholds for Welfare Categories, First Pre–Arab Spring Survey Round
2005 purchasing-power-parity dollars per day

Country/economy	First definition		Second definition with vulnerability line	
	40th percentile	80th percentile	Poor	Vulnerable
Egypt, Arab Rep.	2.5	4.3	2.0	4.9
Jordan	4.3	7.6	2.0	4.9
Syrian Arab Rep.	2.0	3.6	2.0	4.9
Tunisia	4.2	9.1	2.0	4.9
West Bank and Gaza	6.5	13.6	2.0	4.9
Yemen, Rep.	2.3	4.5	2.0	4.9
Average	3.6	7.1	2.0	4.9

Source: Dang and Ianchovichina 2016, using household survey expenditure data.
Note: All estimates are obtained using population weights, except the regional average, which is a simple average. Household heads' age is between 25 and 55 in the first survey round and adjusted accordingly for the second survey round.

at PPP\$2/day is close to the economy-wide absolute poverty thresholds for some of the most populous economies in the sample, Syria and Egypt, although it is higher than the economy-wide absolute poverty lines in the Republic of Yemen and less than the economy-wide poverty lines in Jordan, Tunisia, and the West Bank and Gaza. Therefore, it overestimates poverty in the Republic of Yemen, but it underestimates poverty in Jordan, Tunisia, and the West Bank and Gaza. In all economies, poverty rates, defined at \$2/day (in 2005 PPP\$), were much higher than extreme poverty rates, defined at \$1.25/day. The average extreme poverty rate was low and dropped to less than 2 percent between 2005 and 2011, while the poverty rate at \$2.00/day averaged 16 to 17 percent in the developing MENA region before the Arab Spring. The big difference between the extreme poverty line and the \$2/day poverty line suggests that in many Arab countries a large share of the poor were clustered just above the absolute poverty line of \$1.25/day. This definition implies that the low-income group represents the poor, the middle-income group captures the vulnerable (and perhaps some of the lower middle class), and the top-income group depicts mostly the middle class in Arab countries.

Estimates of the population shares for each income group obtained using the vulnerability line are shown in table 2.2. Before the Arab Spring, the size of the middle class differed substantially across Arab economies, but, on average, about 36 percent of the regional population had middle-income status.[8] The middle class was smallest in Egypt and Syria, where it accounted for between 10 and 15 percent of the population; and it was largest in Tunisia and the West Bank and Gaza, where the majority of the population belonged to the middle class.

TABLE 2.2

Population Shares, by Welfare Category Using Vulnerability Line, First Pre–Arab Spring Survey Round

Country/economy	Poor	Vulnerable	Middle class
West Bank and Gaza	1.4	23.0	75.5
Jordan	4.3	46.2	49.5
Tunisia	9.4	39.9	50.7
Egypt, Arab Rep.	20.2	65.5	14.3
Yemen, Rep.	32.2	50.7	17.0
Syrian Arab Rep.	40.5	50.6	8.9
Average	18.0	46.0	36.0

Source: Dang and Ianchovichina 2016, using household survey expenditure data in the first period.
Note: All estimates are obtained using population weights, except for the regional average, which is a simple average. Household heads' age is between 25 and 55 in the first period (survey round) and adjusted accordingly for the second one. The poverty and vulnerability lines are set at $2/day and $4.9/day, respectively, and the vulnerability line corresponds to a vulnerability index of 20 percent.

Synthetic Panel Method

The analysis of income mobility and welfare dynamics requires panel household survey data, which, unfortunately, are unavailable for the Arab countries.[9] For this reason, this investigation relies on the same set of harmonized household surveys for six Arab economies, presented in table 1.1 and used in chapter 1, and on synthetic panel methods designed specifically to overcome the lack of actual panel data and developed by Dang et al. (2014) and Dang and Lanjouw (2013) for use with repeated cross-sectional data. These methods differ from the literature on pseudo-panel data in two major ways—as few as two rounds of repeated cross sections are required to construct the synthetic panels, and these panels are created at a more disaggregated level than pseudo panels. Because pseudo panels are very data-demanding and require multiple rounds of cross sections (usually 10 rounds or more), and multiple rounds of data are not available for any of the MENA countries in the report, pseudo panels could not be used; synthetic panel techniques were used instead. The synthetic panel methods are broadly related to the literature on survey-to-census imputation (see, for example, Elbers, Lanjouw, and Lanjouw 2003) and survey-to-survey imputation (see, for example, Dang, Lanjouw, and Serajuddin 2014).[10]

A model of income (or consumption), y_{ij}, is estimated from cross-sectional data in survey round j ($j = 1$ or 2), using a specification that includes a vector of household characteristics, x_{ij}, that can be inferred for the other round for household i, $i = 1,…, N$.

$$y_{ij} = \beta_j{}' x_{ij} + \varepsilon_{ij} \qquad (2.1)$$

These household characteristics include variables that may be roughly categorized into three types: (1) time-invariant variables such as ethnicity, religion, place of birth, or parental education; (2) deterministic variables, such as age, that can be computed given the value in one survey round and the time interval between the two survey rounds;[11] and (3) time-varying household characteristics if retrospective questions about the values of such characteristics in the first survey round ($j = 1$) are asked in the second round ($j = 2$). Results of the estimations are shown in appendix 1 in Dang and Ianchovichina (2016).

If z_j is the poverty line in period j, then we are interested in estimating the percentage of households that are poor in the first (or previous) period but nonpoor in the second (or current) period

$$P(y_{i1} < z_1 \text{ and } y_{i2} > z_2), \tag{2.2a}$$

as well as the percentage of poor households in the first period that escape poverty in the second period

$$P(y_{i2} > z_2 \mid y_{i1} < z_1). \tag{2.2b}$$

For the average household, the quantity derived from expression (2.2a) provides the joint (unconditional) probability of household poverty status in both periods, and the quantity derived from expression (2.2b) defines the conditional probability of a household's poverty status in the second period given its poverty status in the first period. Put differently, using panel data, quantities (2.2a) and (2.2b) provide the gross changes of poverty over time, adding a dynamic and more nuanced picture to the net change of poverty than the one that can simply be obtained by comparing the headcount poverty rates in two cross sections.

If true panel data are available, the quantities in expressions (2.2a) and (2.2b) can be estimated in a straightforward way; but in the absence of such data, synthetic panels can be used to study mobility. Two standard assumptions are made, as discussed in box 2.1. In practice, making these assumptions helps operationalize the estimation framework, but formal statistical tests may not result in the satisfaction of these assumptions in every context. For example, the assumption of normal distribution of the error terms is rather standard and commonly made in modeling household consumption data, but this assumption is often failed by formal tests.[12,13]

Quantity (2.2a) can then be estimated by

$$P(y_{i1} < z_1 \text{ and } y_{i2} > z_2) = \Phi_2\left(\frac{z_1 - \beta_1'\mathbf{x}_{i2}}{\sigma_{\varepsilon_1}}, -\frac{z_2 - \beta_2'\mathbf{x}_{i2}}{\sigma_{\varepsilon_2}}, -\rho\right), \tag{2.3}$$

where $\Phi_2(.)$ stands for the bivariate normal cumulative distribution function. In equation (2.3), the parameters β_j and $\sigma_{\varepsilon j}$ are estimated from

---

BOX 2.1

Assumptions Underpinning the Synthetic Panel Approach

The synthetic panel approach is operationalized using two standard assumptions. The first assumption (assumption 1) requires that the underlying populations being sampled in survey rounds 1 and 2 be identical such that their time-invariant characteristics remain the same over time. Coupled with equation (2.1) in the text, this assumption implies that the conditional distribution of expenditure in a given period remains unchanged whether it is conditioned on the given household characteristics in period 1 or period 2, that is, $x_{i1} = x_{i2}$ implies that $y_{i1} | x_{i1}$ and $y_{i1} | x_{i2}$ have identical distributions.

The second assumption (assumption 2) requires that ε_{i1} and ε_{i2} have bivariate normal distributions with positive correlation coefficient ρ and standard deviations ε_{i1} and ε_{i2}, respectively. Then,

$$P(y_{i1} < z_1 \cap y_{i2} > z_2) = \Phi_2\left(\frac{z_1 - \beta_1' x_{i2}}{\sigma_{\varepsilon_1}}, -\frac{z_2 - \beta_2' x_{i2}}{\sigma_{\varepsilon_2}}, -\rho\right), \qquad \text{(B2.1.1)}$$

$$P(y_{i2} > z_2 | y_{i1} < z_1) = \frac{\Phi_2\left(\dfrac{z_1 - \beta_1' x_{i2}}{\sigma_{\varepsilon_1}}, -\dfrac{z_2 - \beta_2' x_{i2}}{\sigma_{\varepsilon_2}}, -\rho\right)}{\Phi\left(\dfrac{z_1 - \beta_1' x_{i2}}{\sigma_{\varepsilon_1}}\right)}. \qquad \text{(B2.1.2)}$$

In equalities (B.2.1.1) and (B.2.1.2), $\Phi_2(.)$ stands for the bivariate normal cumulative distribution function; $\Phi(.)$ stands for the univariate normal cumulative distribution function; the parameters β_j and $\sigma_{\varepsilon j}$ are estimated from equation (2.1); and ρ is estimated using an approximation of cohort-aggregated household consumption between the two surveys.

Dang and Ianchovichina (2016) extend the approach to analyze mobility across three income categories by defining another income threshold, v_j, that specifies the expenditure level above which a person moves into the top income category. In this case, the percentage of poor households in the lowest income category in the first period that escape poverty and move to the group of vulnerable but nonpoor citizens in the second period (joint probability) is:

$$P(y_{i1} < z_1 \cap z_2 < y_{i2} < v_2) = \Phi_2\left(\frac{z_1 - \beta_1' x_{i2}}{\sigma_{\varepsilon_1}}, \frac{v_2 - \beta_2' x_{i2}}{\sigma_{\varepsilon_2}}, \rho\right)$$
$$- \Phi_2\left(\frac{z_1 - \beta_1' x_{i2}}{\sigma_{\varepsilon_1}}, \frac{z_2 - \beta_2' x_{i2}}{\sigma_{\varepsilon_2}}, \rho\right). \qquad \text{(B2.1.3)}$$

equation (2.1), and ρ can be estimated using an approximation of cohort-aggregated household consumption between the two surveys. For prediction purposes, the estimated parameters obtained from data in both survey rounds are applied to data from the second survey round (x_2) (or the base year), but data from the first survey round can be used as well. It is then a straightforward procedure to estimate quantity (2.2b) by dividing quantity (2.2a) by $\Phi\left(\dfrac{z_1 - \beta_1'x_{i2}}{\sigma_{\varepsilon_1}}\right)$, where $\Phi(.)$ stands for the univariate normal cumulative distribution function. To gain further insight into the nature of poverty mobility, the poverty rate in the second period can be decomposed as follows:

$$P(y_{i2} \le Z_2) = P(y_{i1} \le Z_1 \text{ and } y_{i2} \le Z_2) + P(y_{i1} > Z_1 \text{ and } y_{i2} \le Z_2) \qquad (2.4)$$

The first and second terms on the right-hand side of equation (2.4) represent the rate of chronic poverty and downward mobility, respectively. If the poverty rate stays constant between the first and second periods, equation (2.4) implies an inverse relationship between chronic poverty and downward mobility.

Welfare Dynamics

In the period preceding the Arab Spring, poverty rates declined in Jordan, Syria, Tunisia, and the West Bank and Gaza and increased in Egypt and the Republic of Yemen. However, to gain further insight into the nature of poverty dynamics, table 2.3 presents a decomposition of poverty in the

TABLE 2.3

Pre–Arab Spring Changes in Poverty over Time
percent

Country/economy	Headcount in period 1 (1)	Chronically poor (2)	Downwardly mobile (3)	Headcount in period 2 (4) = (2) + (3)	Net change in headcount (5) = (4) − (1)	Upwardly mobile (6)
West Bank and Gaza	1.4	0.1	0.6	0.7	−0.7	1.3
Jordan	4.3	1.0	1.4	2.4	−1.9	3.3
Tunisia	9.4	1.2	3.7	4.9	−4.5	8.2
Syrian Arab Rep.	40.5	7.3	1.1	8.4	−32.1	33.2
Egypt, Arab Rep.	20.2	13.3	15.9	29.2	9.0	6.9
Yemen, Rep.	32.3	28.3	27.5	55.8	23.4	4.0
Average	18.0	8.5	8.3	16.9	−1.1	9.5

Source: Dang and Ianchovichina 2016.

Note: All estimates are obtained using population weights, except for the regional average, which is a simple average. Household heads' age is between 25 and 55 in the first period and adjusted accordingly in the second period. The poverty line is set at $2 a day in 2005 purchasing-power-parity dollars in both periods. Estimates for chronic poverty are based on the synthetic panels. The time length between the first and second periods varies by economy. It is longest for Syria and the Republic of Yemen (six to seven years) and shortest for Jordan (two years); in all other cases the time period spans three to four years.

second period into chronic poverty and downward mobility as well as upward mobility between the two periods. According to these estimates, poverty dynamics were mostly positive before the Arab Spring. Slightly more than half (53 percent) of the poor in the first period moved out of poverty in the second period, but chronic poverty remained high in Egypt and the Republic of Yemen. Egypt, Syria, and the Republic of Yemen had the highest poverty incidence in the region, but unlike Syria poverty rates increased in the Republic of Yemen and Egypt.

Next, the welfare dynamics for the three welfare categories or income groups—the low-income group, the middle-income group, and the top-income group, shown in tables 2.4 and 2.5 for the two definitions,

TABLE 2.4

Pre–Arab Spring Changes in the Size of Welfare Categories Defined Using the First Definition

percent

| Country/economy | Growth in the population share of each welfare category | | | Annual growth in mean consumption |
	Bottom 40%	Middle 40%	Top 20%	
Syrian Arab Rep.	−79.8	−21.2	202.0	10.1
Tunisia	−32.2	14.4	35.6	2.9
West Bank and Gaza	−11.0	9.0	4.0	1.2
Jordan	−0.7	2.2	−3.0	−0.8
Egypt, Arab Rep.	28.0	−13.7	−28.5	−2.7
Yemen, Rep.	58.5	−31.9	−53.2	−3.7
Average	−6.2	−6.9	26.2	1.2

Source: Dang and Ianchovichina 2016.
Note: All estimates are obtained using population weights, except for the regional average, which is a simple average. Household heads' age is between 25 and 55 in the first survey round and adjusted accordingly for the second survey round. The first definition uses the 40th and 80th percentiles of the income distribution in the first period to set the thresholds that respectively identify the bottom 40 percent and the middle 40 percent in both periods.

TABLE 2.5

Pre–Arab Spring Changes in the Size of Welfare Categories Defined Using the Second Definition

percent

| Country/economy | Growth in the population share of each welfare category | | | Annual growth in mean consumption |
	Poor	Vulnerable	Middle class	
Syrian Arab Rep.	−79.4	3.1	343.2	10.1
Tunisia	−48.0	−21.7	26.0	2.9
West Bank and Gaza	−48.4	−17.0	6.1	1.2
Jordan	−44.7	1.6	2.4	−0.8
Egypt, Arab Rep.	44.6	−7.0	−31.1	−2.7
Yemen, Rep.	72.6	−28.7	−52.5	−3.7
Average	−6.2	−11.6	49.0	1.2

Source: Dang and Ianchovichina 2016.
Note: All estimates are obtained using population weights, except for the regional average, which is a simple average. Household heads' age is between 25 and 55 in the first survey round and adjusted accordingly for the second survey round. The poverty and vulnerability lines are set at $2.0/day and $4.9/day, respectively. The second definition uses a vulnerability line that corresponds to a vulnerability index of 20 percent.

are broadly consistent with the poverty dynamics discussed in table 2.3. In particular, in Egypt and the Republic of Yemen, consumption growth was negative, on average, and the ranks of the middle and top income groups declined whereas those of the poor expanded considerably. Yet, in the remaining economies, a more nuanced picture of welfare dynamics emerges. In Syria and Tunisia, the size of the low-income group declined, the size of the top-income group expanded, and the ranks of the middle-income group either declined or increased (table 2.4 and table 2.5).[14]

Upward mobility was stronger than downward mobility in Syria and Tunisia, but the reverse was the case in Egypt and the Republic of Yemen, whereas in Jordan upward and downward mobility were in greater balance (figure 2.1). Welfare dynamics were most sluggish in Egypt and the Republic of Yemen, where the share of those who did not change income categories (that is, the immobile) was largest (figure 2.1). People with no education, those employed as informal workers, and those living in rural areas appear to have had lower-than-average chances for upward mobility before the Arab Spring (panel a of figure 2.2).[15] These are also the same characteristics associated with having higher-than-average chances of downward mobility (panel b of figure 2.2), while the opposite holds for the remaining characteristics.[16]

Overall, at the regional level, the middle class or those relatively unlikely to fall into poverty grew from 36 percent of the population in the first period (late 1990s or early 2000s) (table 2.2) to 42 percent in the second period (mid- to late 2000s) (table 2.6). In most Arab

FIGURE 2.1

Pre–Arab Spring Welfare Dynamics across Income Groups, by Economy

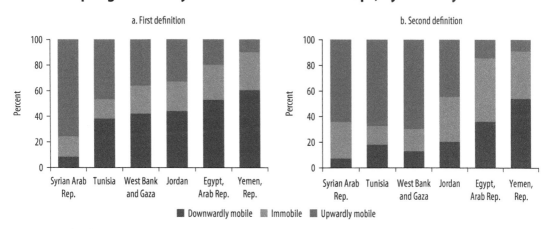

Source: Dang and Ianchovichina 2016.

FIGURE 2.2

Region-Wide Welfare Dynamics Using Monetary Measures by Population Group, before 2010

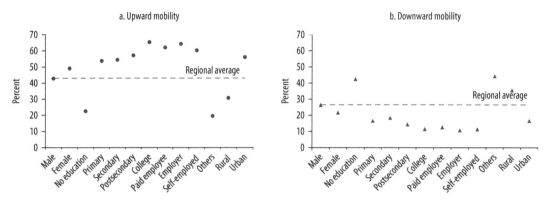

Source: Dang and Ianchovichina 2016.
Note: "Others" includes the unemployed, informal workers, unpaid family workers, and the rest of the employment status categories.

TABLE 2.6

Population Shares by Welfare Category Using Vulnerability Line, Second Pre–Arab Spring Survey Round Period

percent

Country or economy	Poor	Vulnerable	Middle class
West Bank and Gaza	0.7	19.1	80.1
Jordan	2.4	46.9	50.7
Tunisia	4.9	31.3	63.8
Syrian Arab Rep.	8.4	52.2	39.4
Egypt, Arab Rep.	29.2	61.0	9.8
Yemen, Rep.	55.8	36.2	8.0
Average	16.0	41.1	42.0

Source: Dang and Ianchovichina (2016) using household survey expenditure data.
Note: All estimates are obtained using population weights, except for the regional average, which is a simple average. Household heads' age is between 25 and 55 in the first survey round and adjusted accordingly for the second one. The poverty and vulnerability lines are set at $2.0/day and $4.9/day, respectively, and the vulnerability line corresponds to a vulnerability index of 20 percent.

economies, the size of the middle class increased and the size of the low-income groups declined, except in Egypt and the Republic of Yemen, where the reverse occurred. However, in nearly all developing Arab economies, and especially in the Arab Spring countries (Egypt, Libya, Syria, Tunisia, and the Republic of Yemen), the consumption of the middle class either declined or lagged behind that of other groups (table 2.7). In Tunisia, where the Arab Spring started, upward mobility

TABLE 2.7

Pre–Arab Spring Annual Growth in Mean Consumption, by Welfare Category

percent

Country or economy	Bottom 40%	Middle 40%	Top 20%
Syrian Arab Rep.	14.9	5.7	31.5
Tunisia	5.1	2.4	−5.4
West Bank and Gaza	3.8	−0.3	2.2
Jordan	2.0	−0.7	−2.8
Egypt, Arab Rep.	−4.0	−1.6	−1.5
Yemen, Rep.	−10.3	−3.8	17.3
Average	1.9	0.3	6.3

Source: Dang and Ianchovichina 2016.
Note: The 40th and 80th percentiles of the income distribution in the first period are used as the thresholds that respectively identify the bottom 40 percent and the middle 40 percent for both periods.

was stronger than downward mobility, but the consumption of the middle class (the top 60 percent) grew, on average, at a lower rate than the consumption of the bottom 40 percent. Inequality declined as the expenditure of affluent households (the top 20 percent) contracted by more than 5 percent and that of the bottom 40 percent increased by the same percentage. In Egypt, all segments of the population compressed their spending. In the Republic of Yemen, the consumption of the affluent and the upper-middle class increased by slightly more than 17 percent, but downward mobility was strong (table 2.4) and inequality increased. In Syria, the spending of the affluent top 20 percent and the poorest bottom 40 percent grew at a higher rate compared with that of the middle 40 percent in the period between the mid-1990s and the mid-2000s.

In summary, the empirical evidence presented in this chapter suggests that the middle class in many developing Arab countries was getting squeezed. This was certainly the case in Egypt and the Republic of Yemen, where welfare dynamics were negative as many people either lost or struggled to retain their middle-income status. Elsewhere in developing MENA, the ranks of the middle class grew but the incomes of the middle class either declined (Jordan, the West Bank and Gaza), grew at a lower rate than the incomes of the poor (Tunisia), or did not grow as fast as the incomes of the most affluent (in Syria). In addition, as presented in the next chapter, subjective welfare measures indicate that, on the eve of the Arab Spring, the majority of Arab people in developing MENA were frustrated, and dissatisfaction rates rose, especially toward the end of the first decade of the 2000s.

Notes

1. These definitions have been proposed in studies by Ravallion (2010), Birdsall (2007), Chun (2010), African Development Bank (2011), Ferreira et al. (2013), and Kharas (2013).
2. The middle class can be defined in different ways, each offering advantages and disadvantages. This study relies on operationally straightforward definitions that enable comparisons across countries (at very different stages of development) and time. Definitions using occupation or education level are also useful. Therefore, this inquiry also looks at welfare changes for specific population groups, distinguished by gender, educational attainment, type of employment, and location.
3. The terms "income" and "consumption" are used interchangeably in this study. The poor or the bottom 40 percent are referred to as the lowest-income group, the middle 40 percent as the middle-income group, and the top 20 percent as the top-income group.
4. See Dang and Lanjouw (2015) for more details.
5. The bottom 40 percent of the region-wide income distribution could be considered, but may not add much value to country-level analysis because income levels differ substantially across countries in the MENA region.
6. The household surveys cover different years for different countries (table 1.1).
7. Abu-Ismail and Sarangi (2013) estimate the lower poverty line, also known as the food poverty line, at 2005 PPP$2.3 a day in 2011, and construct an upper poverty line that includes expenditure on food and essential nonfood items.
8. The regional averages are simple (unweighted) averages. The middle class increases to slightly more than 40 percent of the regional population in the second period.
9. Even when such panel surveys exist, they are often plagued by data quality issues such as attrition bias due to the fact that some households drop out of the sample in follow-up survey rounds.
10. Recent applications or validations of synthetic panel methods against actual panel data include Bierbaum and Gassmann (2012) for the Kyrgyz Republic, Ferreira et al. (2013) and Cruces et al. (2015) for Latin American countries, Martinez et al. (2013) for the Philippines, Garbero (2014) for Vietnam, Cancho et al. (2015) for European and Central Asian countries, and Dang and Lanjouw (2015) for India.
11. To reduce spurious changes caused by changes in household composition over time, the estimation samples are restricted to household heads ages 25 to 55 in the first cross section; this age range is adjusted accordingly in the second cross section. This restriction also helps ensure that certain variables such as household heads' educational attainment remain relatively stable over time, assuming these household heads are finished with their schooling. This age range is usually used in traditional pseudo-panel analysis but can vary depending on the cultural and economic factors in each specific setting. Headcount poverty rates without the age restriction (table 1.1) are very similar to those with this restriction (table 2.3) (Dang and Ianchovichina 2016).

12. In addition, a formal test of the bivariate normal distribution for assumption 2 in box 2.1 would require actual panel data. In the absence of such data, one can only implement a partial test for assumption 2 with a test for the univariate normal distribution for the two cross sections. More important, the ultimate test is whether the estimates for poverty dynamics based on the synthetic panels can reasonably approximate those based on the actual panel data. See Dang and Lanjouw (2013) and Dang et al. (2014) for further discussion of these assumptions; asymptotic results and formulas for the standard errors are provided in Dang and Lanjouw (2013).

13. One useful way to check on both assumptions 1 and 2 in box 2.1 (as well as the overall fit of the estimation model) is to use both the survey rounds separately as the base year and then compare estimation results. Dang and Ianchovichina (2016) show that varying the base year leads to similar estimates.

14. Note that the results for the West Bank and Gaza should be interpreted with caution because much of the expenditure growth is driven by foreign aid rather than by sustainable economic activity.

15. Figure 2.2 displays the percentage of the poor or vulnerable in the first period who move up one or two welfare categories in the second period for major population groups classified by gender; education level (less than primary [or no] education, primary education, secondary education, postsecondary education, and college); occupation (paid employee, employer, self-employed, and others, comprising informal work, including unpaid family workers and other categories); and residence areas (rural or urban). This figure and figure 2.1 show conditional, rather than the joint, probabilities because this representation more clearly brings out the transition patterns for the different population groups.

16. Factors that are positively correlated with upward mobility are, in general, related to those associated with escaping downward mobility, but this may not always hold. See, for example, Dang and Lanjouw (2015) for an analysis of mobility in India.

References

Abu-Ismail, K., and N. Sarangi. 2013. "A New Approach to Measuring the Middle Class: Egypt." ESCWA Working Paper, United Nations, New York.

African Development Bank. 2011. "The Middle of the Pyramid: Dynamics of the Middle Class in Africa." *Market Brief*, April.

Ali, A. G. A. 2011. "Middle Class in the Arab Countries." *Development Bridge* 103. Kuwait: API (May).

Basu, K. 2013. "Shared Prosperity and the Mitigation of Poverty: In Practice and in Precept." Policy Research Working Paper 6700, World Bank, Washington, DC.

Bierbaum, M., and F. Gassmann. 2012. "Chronic and Transitory Poverty in the Kyrgyz Republic: What Can Synthetic Panels Tell Us?" UNU-MERIT Working Paper 2012-064, UNU-MERIT, Maastricht, Netherlands.

Birdsall, N. 2007. "Reflections on the Macroeconomic Foundations of Inclusive Middle-Class Growth." Center for Global Development Working Paper 130, Center for Global Development, Washington, DC.

Cancho, A. C., M. E. Dávalos, G. Demarchi, M. Meyer, and C. Sánchez Páramo. 2015. "Economic Mobility in Europe and Central Asia: Exploring Patterns and Uncovering Puzzles." Policy Research Working Paper 7173, World Bank, Washington, DC.

Chun, N. 2010. "Middle Class Size in the Past, Present, and Future: A Description of Trends in Asia." Economics Working Paper 217, Asian Development Bank, Manila, Philippines.

Cruces, G., P. Lanjouw, L. Lucchetti, E. Perova, R. Vakis, and M. Viollaz. 2015. "Estimating Poverty Transitions Repeated Cross-Sections: A Three-Country Validation Exercise." *Journal of Economic Inequality* 13: 161–79.

Dang, H., and E. Ianchovichina. 2016. "Welfare Dynamics with Synthetic Panels: The Case of the Arab World in Transition." Policy Research Working Paper 7595, World Bank, Washington, DC.

Dang, H., and P. Lanjouw. 2013. "Measuring Poverty Dynamics with Synthetic Panels Based on Cross-Sections." Policy Research Working Paper 6504, World Bank, Washington, DC.

———. 2015. "Poverty Dynamics in India between 2004–2012: Insights from Longitudinal Analysis Using Synthetic Panel Data." Policy Research Working Paper 7270, World Bank, Washington, DC.

———. 2016a. "Toward a New Definition of Shared Prosperity: A Dynamic Perspective from Three Countries." In *Inequality and Growth: Patterns and Policy*, edited by Kaushik Basu and Joseph Stiglitz. New York: Palgrave Macmillan Press.

———. 2016b. "Welfare Dynamics Measurement: Two Definitions of a Vulnerability Line." *Review of Income and Wealth*, published online.

Dang, H., P. Lanjouw, and U. Serajuddin. 2014. "Updating Poverty Estimates at Frequent Intervals in the Absence of Consumption Data: Methods and Illustration with Reference to a Middle-Income Country." Policy Research Working Paper 7043, World Bank, Washington, DC.

Dang, H., P. Lanjouw, J. Luoto, and D. McKenzie. 2014. "Using Repeated Cross-Sections to Explore Movements in and out of Poverty." *Journal of Development Economics* 107: 112–28.

Deaton, A. 2010. "Price Indexes, Inequality, and the Measurement of World Poverty." *American Economic Review* 100 (1): 5–34.

Easterly, W. 2001. "The Middle Class Consensus and Economic Development." *Journal of Economic Growth* 6 (4): 317–35.

Elbers, C., J. Lanjouw, and P. Lanjouw. 2003. "Micro-Level Estimation of Poverty and Inequality." *Econometrica* 71 (1): 355–64.

Ferreira, F. H. G., J. Messina, J. Rigolini, L. F. López-Calva, M. A. Lugo, and R. Vakis. 2013. *Economic Mobility and the Rise of the Latin American Middle Class.* Washington, DC: World Bank.

Garbero, A. 2014. "Estimating Poverty Dynamics Using Synthetic Panels for IFAD-Supported Projects: A Case Study from Vietnam." *Journal of Development Effectiveness* 6 (4): 490–510.

Kharas, H. 2013. "The Emerging Middle Class in Developing Countries." Working Paper 285, OECD Development Centre, Paris.

Martinez, A., M. Western, M. Haynes, and W. Tomaszewski. 2013. "Measuring Income Mobility Using Pseudo-Panel Data." *Philippine Statistician* 62 (2): 71–99.

Rama, M., T. Béteille, Y. Li, P. Mitra, and J. Newman. 2015. *Addressing Inequality in South Asia*. Washington, DC: World Bank.

Ravallion, M. 2010. "The Developing World's Bulging (but Vulnerable) Middle Class." *World Development* 38 (4): 445–54.

PART 2

The "Unhappy Development" Syndrome

Before the Arab Spring uprising, most countries in the Middle East and North Africa (MENA) region were believed to be stable and relatively prosperous. Absolute poverty rates and inequality levels were low and had been declining for years, and access to education and health services had dramatically improved. With autocratic rulers in power for many years, the cracks in these countries' models of government remained invisible to most observers, including political scientists (Gause 2011); some considered Islam a stabilizing force (Bromley 2014). Yet, the emergence of social discontent in the Arab countries could be detected using subjective well-being data, which is a meaningful and consistent way of measuring people's welfare and shows the importance of taking into account nonmaterial elements to provide a broader picture of well-being when studying poverty and shared prosperity concepts (Clark, Frijters, and Shields 2008).

Life satisfaction in most developing MENA countries was below the average for the group of countries at a similar level of development (figure P2.1) and had dropped significantly in the years before the Arab Spring events (figure P2.2). For the region as a whole inequality in well-being was relatively high, second highest after Latin America and the Caribbean (figure P2.3), unlike the moderate to low levels of monetary inequality (see chapter 1).

The phenomenon of declining levels of happiness during a time of moderate-to-rapid development (figures O.2, O.3, O.5, and P2.2) represents a paradox, defined by Arampatzi et al. (2015) as the "unhappy development" paradox. It is related to the Easterlin (1974) paradox of growth without a corresponding increase in reported happiness levels and to Graham and Lora's (2009) "unhappy growth" paradox. This part of the study aims to shed light on the reasons behind the emergence of this paradox in the Arab countries and argues that the paradox can more accurately

FIGURE P2.1

Satisfaction with Life and GDP per Capita, 2007–10

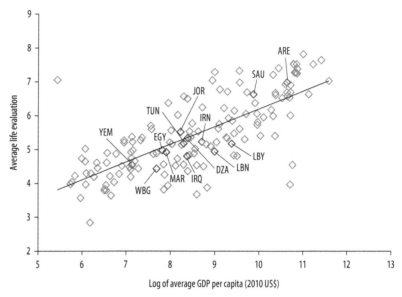

Source: Arampatzi et al. 2015, using World Bank data on gross domestic product (GDP) per capita and Gallup World Poll data on life satisfaction. Log of average GDP per capita: World Bank World Development Indicators; Life evaluation: Gallup World Poll 2012.
Note: Numbers are weighted averages for 124 economies. ARE = United Arab Emirates; DZA = Algeria; EGY = Arab Republic of Egypt; IRN = Islamic Republic of Iran; IRQ = Iraq; JOR = Jordan; LBN = Lebanon; LBY = Libya; MAR = Morocco; SAU = Saudi Arabia; TUN = Tunisia; WBG = West Bank and Gaza; YEM = Republic of Yemen.

FIGURE P2.2

Change in Satisfaction with Life and GDP Growth, 2007–10

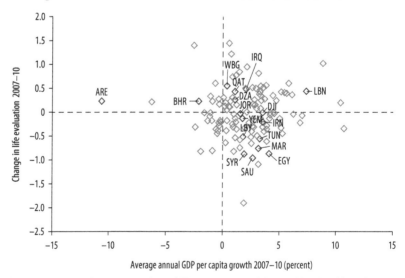

Sources: Arampatzi et al. 2015, using real annual GDP per capita growth from World Bank World Development Indicators and life satisfaction from Gallup World Poll.
Note: Numbers are weighted averages for 124 economies. ARE = United Arab Emirates; BHR = Bahrain; DJI = Djibouti; DZA = Algeria; EGY = Arab Republic of Egypt; IRN = Islamic Republic of Iran; JOR = Jordan; LBN = Lebanon; LBY = Libya; MAR = Morocco; QAT = Qatar; SAU = Saudi Arabia; SYR = Syrian Arab Republic; TUN = Tunisia; WBG = West Bank and Gaza; YEM = Republic of Yemen.

FIGURE P2.3

Inequality in Subjective Well-Being, 2006–09

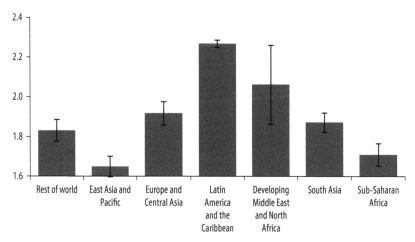

Source: Gallup World Poll data on life satisfaction.
Note: Rest of world = mostly developed countries. Figure shows inequality in average life evaluation measured as standard deviation in life evaluation, shown along with 95 percent confidence intervals.

be characterized as an unhappy development syndrome, reflecting the symptoms of a broken social contract. The analysis allows us to link the reasons for the growing unhappiness to those that compelled people to demonstrate during the Arab Spring events and to link the rise in dissatisfaction rates to demand for change, which was particularly strong in the Arab Spring countries. The "Arab inequality" puzzle is solved by showing that a broken social contract, not high and rising inequality, triggered the Arab Spring. The broken social contract had negative implications for many areas of life; these implications were evident in measurements of individual subjective well-being data, but could not be detected through the standard expenditure data that are regularly used to measure poverty and shared prosperity and that appeal to a critical level of utility from consumption rather than overall satisfaction with life.

References

Arampatzi, E., M. Burger, E. Ianchovichina, T. Röhricht, and R. Veenhoven. 2015. "Unhappy Development: Dissatisfaction with Life on the Eve of the Arab Spring." Policy Research Working Paper 7488, World Bank, Washington, DC.

Bromley, R. 2014. "The 'Arab Spring' Stress Test: Diagnosing Reasons for the Revolt." Working Paper, University of Wisconsin-Madison.

Clark, A. E., P. Frijters, and M. A. Shields. 2008. "Relative Income, Happiness, and Utility: An Explanation for the Easterlin Paradox and Other Puzzles." *Journal of Economic Literature* 46: 95–144.

Easterlin, R. 1974. "Does Economic Growth Improve the Human Lot? Some Empirical Evidence." In *Nations and Households in Economic Growth: Essays in Honor of Moses Abramovitz*, edited by R. David and R. Reder. New York: Academic Press.

Gause III, G. F. 2011. "Why Middle East Studies Missed the Arab Spring." *Foreign Affairs* 90: 81–90.

Graham, C., and E. Lora. 2009. "Happiness and Health Satisfaction across Countries." In *Paradox and Perception: Measuring Quality of Life in Latin America*, edited by C. Graham and E. Lora. Washington, DC: Brookings Institution Press.

CHAPTER 3

Dissatisfaction with Life: Subjective Data Analysis

Introduction

Welfare measures based on consumption or income data from household surveys are widely used for poverty and shared prosperity analyses, but they provide a partial picture of individuals' well-being and have proved to be of limited value in understanding the factors behind the Arab Spring. Greater acceptance of subjective well-being measures, which denote both individual and social welfare (Veenhoven 2012), as a direct proxy for utility has opened up a wide range of opportunities to further inform theory and policy design (Clark, Frijters, and Shields 2008).

In this chapter, analysis based on subjective well-being data enables us to understand the reasons behind the growing popular Arab anger on the eve of the Arab Spring. The main problem with objective measures of welfare, such as household per capita income or expenditure, is that they capture only a fraction of the components of the utility function, those most crucial to measuring poverty rather than overall well-being. When used to measure utility from relative income, these measures are inadequate because the reference level of income evolves over time. Clark, Frijters, and Shields (2008) argue that a happiness-based poverty measure must take into account nonmaterial elements to provide a broader picture of well-being or the lives that individuals live.

Subjective Well-Being versus Monetary Welfare Measures

Various explorations and studies have identified clear positive relationships between happiness and income, marriage, job status, health, and religion (Kahneman, Diener, and Schwarz 1999; Layard 2006).[1]

These findings indicate that deterioration in the quality of public health services and difficulties in finding good-quality jobs would be detrimental to an individual's well-being. Nonmaterial, quality-of-life factors affect the well-being of individuals to a great degree but are not reflected in the monetary measures, such as income and expenditures, regularly used to track individual welfare. Other factors undetected by traditional expenditure data include the quality of education and infrastructure services (for example, electricity, transportation, and administrative government services), the quality of jobs available in the economy, environmental and institutional quality, public safety, control of corruption, the fairness of the justice system, and political and economic stability, among others.

In addition, objective indicators may not provide a complete picture of the economic developments that may affect the well-being of individuals in a country. For example, rather than improved well-being, an increase in expenditure-based measures of welfare may simply signal that households have increased their spending on private sector services because of the deteriorating quality of public services. This situation may occur during periods of fiscal compression and public sector budget cuts, and it may lead people to adopt a variety of coping mechanisms, including depleting their private savings, increasing their debt, or working multiple jobs. Of course, all these choices reduce the subjective well-being of individuals.

However, the link between happiness and utility needs to be approached with caution. Happiness is an evaluation of what has happened and is not the same as what people expect to happen in the future. If individuals make systematic mistakes in predicting their happiness, there will be a difference between happiness and decision utility as argued by Kahneman, Wakker, and Sarin (1997). According to Rabin (1998) this happens because people underestimate how quickly they will adapt to changes in their reference points. Preferences and expectations change over time as people calibrate their subjective well-being according to the "ideal" they have for their personal lives (the reference point) and according either to changes in domains important to their happiness (for example, perceptions of government become more positive) or the importance of these domains for their personal well-being (for example, trust in government becomes more important to people's quality of life).[2]

Apart from the known malleability of happiness scores (Bertrand and Mullainathan 2001), using them as a welfare measure may also result in problems because of the argument that there is more to life than happiness. As argued by Kimball and Willis (2006), people may trade off happiness against other constituent parts of utility such as autonomy, competence, personal growth, positive relationships, self-acceptance, engagement, and meaning (Deci and Ryan 2000; Ryff 1989; Ryff and Singer 1998; Seligman 2002). However, it can be argued that these areas are central not only to utility but also to individual happiness although the links may be indirect. Achieving personal autonomy may require sacrifices that reduce happiness in the current period, but greater freedom in decision making may bring opportunities that increase happiness in the next period. Therefore, despite these caveats, this part of the study argues that a strong case can be made for using subjective well-being measures to study the economics of the Arab Spring. The remainder of this chapter turns to the definition of happiness, how it is measured for the purposes of this study, and what these measures tell us about happiness or the lack of it in the Arab countries.

Measuring Life Satisfaction

Happiness is defined as "the degree to which an individual judges the overall quality of his/her own life-as-a-whole favorably" (Veenhoven 1984, 22) and it is often used interchangeably with "subjective well-being," "life satisfaction," or "quality of life."[3] Subjective well-being is often measured using the Cantril ladder scores,[4] which are part of the Gallup World Poll and are available for 150 countries representing more than 98 percent of the world's population. Cantril's (1965) Self-Anchoring Striving Scale (Cantril Scale) asks survey respondents to imagine a ladder with steps numbered from zero at the bottom to 10 at the top. The top of the ladder represents the best possible life for the particular respondent and the bottom of the ladder represents the worst possible life for the respondent. Respondents are then asked to determine on which step of the ladder they personally feel they stand at this time.

Changes in individual Cantril Scale scores over time can be due to changes in the reference point, objective circumstances, expectations, and uncertainty or to a combination of changes in all of these factors. Used widely by researchers, the Cantril Scale measures of well-being have been found to be closer to the end of the continuum representing life evaluations (Diener et al. 2009); and, in contrast to measures of feelings or affect, the Cantril Scale life evaluations have been found to be closely correlated with income (Deaton 2008).

Analysis using data sets with hundreds of thousands of respondents have determined a pattern in the Cantril Scale data in the Gallup World Poll. These data suggest at least three distinct categories of life evaluations formed by (1) thriving people with well-being scores of 7 or above, (2) struggling individuals with scores between 4 and 7, and (3) suffering people with scores of 4 or below. Thriving people report significantly fewer health problems; fewer sick days; less worry, stress, sadness, and anger; and more respect. They are mostly happy or satisfied with their lives so we refer to them as the group of happy or *satisfied* people. Struggling people report more daily stress and worry about money than do thriving respondents and more than double the amount of sick days. They are more likely to smoke and less likely to eat healthily than are thriving individuals. Suffering people are likely to report poor health, physical pain, lack of food and shelter, stress issues, worry, sadness, and anger. They are also likely to have limited access to health insurance and care. Because struggling people are unhappy and dissatisfied with their lives, we refer to them as the group of unhappy or *dissatisfied* people. In Denmark fewer than 1 percent of all people can be considered suffering, whereas in Zimbabwe 40 percent of people fall into this category. Typically, the share of suffering individuals in the population is highly correlated with measures of poverty.

How satisfied people are with their lives depends on objective conditions and subjective factors, including perceptions and expectations. According to Layard (2006), objective factors such as gender, age, marital and educational status, financial situation, and health to a large extent determine individual happiness; but subjective factors associated with perceptions and expectations about family relationships, work, community and friends, personal freedom, institutional quality, and personal values are also imperative to individual happiness. These domains of life reflect the most important human needs as identified by Maslow (1943). The relative importance of the objective and subjective determinants of life satisfaction vary over time and across individuals.

By relying on the Cantril ladder scores rather than on indexes that reflect index makers' opinions of what matters most,[5] this study gives voice to the people and places primary importance on people's evaluations of their own lives. The responses of surveyed respondents include both monetary and nonmonetary factors affecting subjective well-being and therefore can be used in analyses aimed at understanding the value people attach to a comprehensive set of factors and circumstances that affect their lives and contribute to their unhappiness.[6]

Dissatisfaction with Life in Arab Countries

The study uses the Cantril ladder scores from the Gallup World Poll surveys, which are available for nearly all developing Arab countries, including Algeria, the Arab Republic of Egypt, Iraq, Jordan, Lebanon, Morocco, the Syrian Arab Republic, Tunisia, and the Republic of Yemen, during the period 2009–12.[7] On the eve of the Arab Spring, average subjective well-being levels in most Arab economies were lower than those expected for their income levels, especially in Syria, the West Bank and Gaza, Lebanon, the Republic of Yemen, and Libya (figure P2.1). The distribution of life evaluation scores in the developing countries of the Middle East and North Africa (MENA) region in the period before the Arab Spring was skewed toward the categories of "struggling" and "suffering" people, that is, those whose life satisfaction scores were 7 or below (figure 3.1). Region-wide, nearly two-thirds of people had life evaluation scores of 5 or lower, and only 10 percent of the population was satisfied and had a score of 8 or higher. The percentage of people dissatisfied with their lives varied by country within MENA (figure 3.2), but in all Arab Spring countries the share of those "suffering" and "struggling" surpassed 80 percent in 2010, the year of the Arab Spring (figure 3.2, panel a).

Individual Arab countries exhibited substantial differences in the average life satisfaction levels of the different welfare groups, yet in most cases, as expected, subjective well-being was positively associated with the income level of the welfare group (figure 3.3). This regularity, however, did not hold in 2010 in three of the Arab Spring countries (Egypt, Libya, and Syria). In Egypt, the group of vulnerable people (those in the second quintile of the income distribution) and the lower middle class (the third quintile) had similar levels of life satisfaction, averaging 4.5 in

FIGURE 3.1

Distribution of Individual Life Satisfaction Scores in Developing MENA, 2009–10

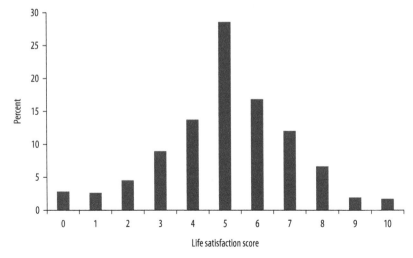

Source: Arampatzi et al. 2015, using Gallup World Poll data.
Note: MENA = Middle East and North Africa.

FIGURE 3.2

Distribution of Life Satisfaction, by Economy

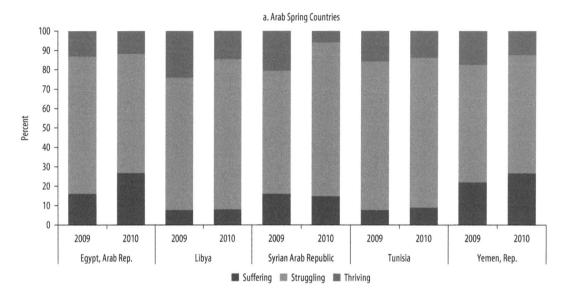

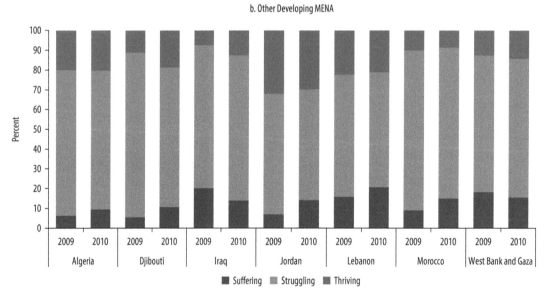

Source: Data from Gallup World Poll.
Note: MENA = Middle East and North Africa.

2010 (figure 3.3). In Syria and Libya, life satisfaction in 2010 was uniformly low across all income quintiles (figure 3.3).

Happiness levels were generally lower for those living in rural areas than for those living in urban centers. Differences in average life evaluation levels were particularly pronounced at the two extreme ends of the distribution, that is, the poor and the affluent (figure 3.4). However, the regional scores hide important differences across countries. In Egypt, all people in urban areas were less satisfied with their lives than those living in rural areas, except the rich who lived happier lives in the cities than in the rural areas of Egypt. In Tunisia, Syria and the Republic of Yemen,

FIGURE 3.3

Average Life Evaluation, by Welfare Group and Country

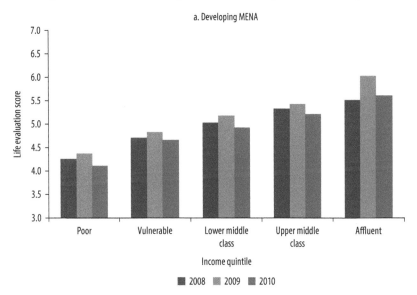

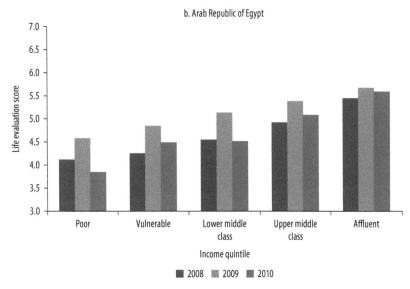

(continued on next page)

FIGURE 3.3

Average Life Evaluation, by Welfare Group and Country   *Continued*

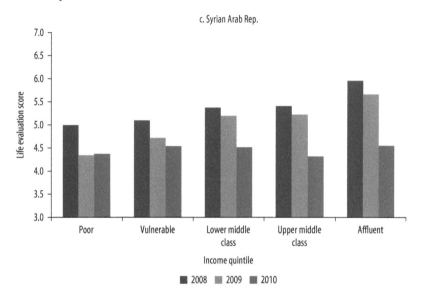

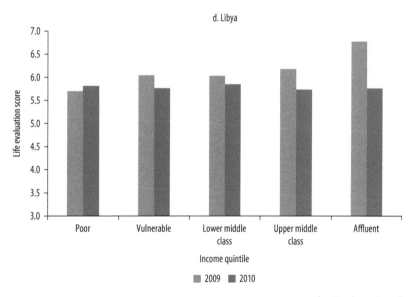

(continued on next page)

FIGURE 3.3

Average Life Evaluation, by Welfare Group and Country *Continued*

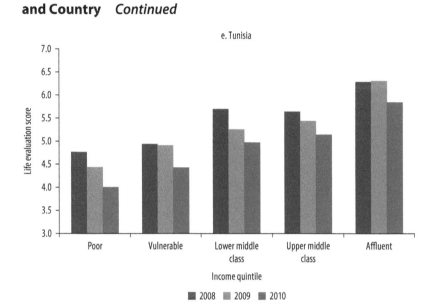

e. Tunisia

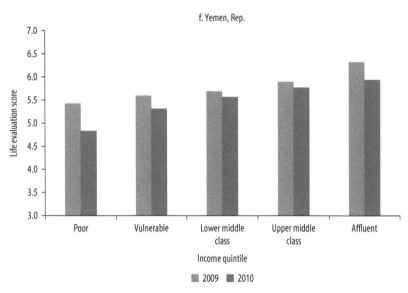

f. Yemen, Rep.

Source: Data from Gallup World Poll.
Note: MENA = Middle East and North Africa. There were no data for 2008 for Libya and the Republic of Yemen.

FIGURE 3.4

Average Life Evaluation, by Income Class and Location, 2009–10

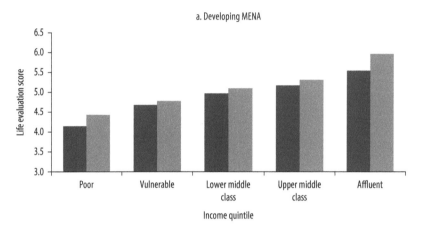

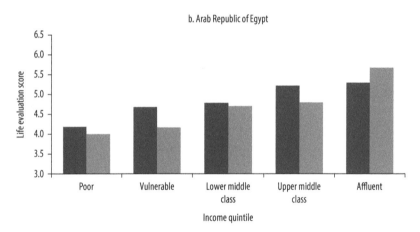

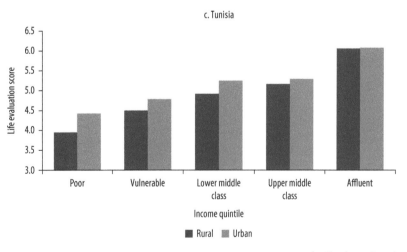

(continued on next page)

FIGURE 3.4

Average Life Evaluation, by Income Class and Location, 2009–10 *Continued*

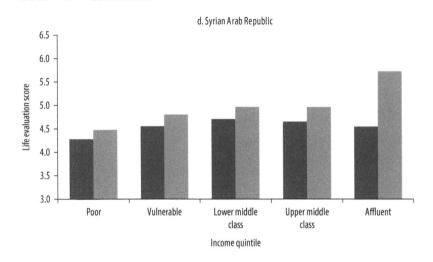

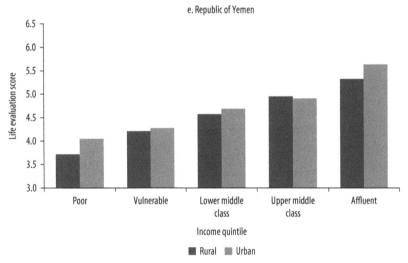

Source: Data from Gallup World Poll.
Note: MENA = Middle East and North Africa. There were no data for Libya.

urban dwellers were happier than rural residents. In Syria, the difference in happiness levels of affluent urban and rural residents is striking and suggests that people in rural areas were uniformly dissatisfied regardless of income status. This low level of rural residents' well-being is consistent with evidence that many rural areas in these countries were neglected and underserved, and in Syria it also reflects the consequences of the drought in the second half of the decade when, according to experts, up to 60 percent of Syria's land experienced its worst-ever long-term drought and most severe set of crop failures (Femia and Werrell 2012).

Consistent with perceptions that public sector jobs are better than private sector jobs because they offer security and benefits, public sector workers were, on average, happier than private sector employees in 2009; these differences in life satisfaction levels widened in 2010 (figure 3.5).[8] In all countries, blue collar workers were, on average, less happy than white collar workers; and they, in turn, were less happy than business owners. In 2010, however, business owners were less happy than white or

FIGURE 3.5

Average Life Evaluation, by Country, Type of Job, and Occupation

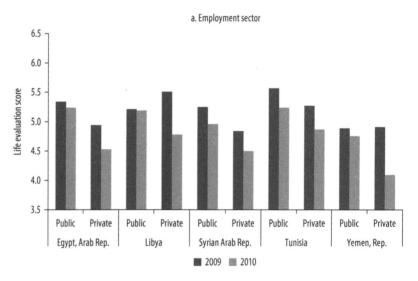

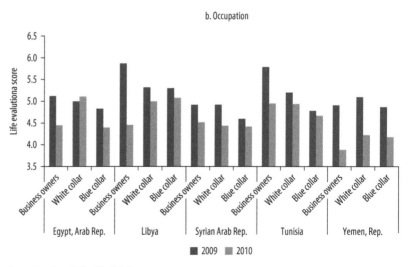

Source: Data from Gallup World Poll.

blue collar workers in Egypt, Libya, and the Republic of Yemen. In Tunisia, happiness levels among business owners declined significantly and became comparable to those of white collar workers; and, in Syria, life satisfaction levels were uniformly low across different types of occupations.

The next chapter explores welfare dynamics with subjective data and compares the evolution of subjective well-being before the Arab Spring with the evolution of objective welfare measures in each country for which information is available. These comparisons, although not strict because of differences in the available survey years for the Gallup World Poll and household data at the country level, suggest that objective statistics provide a partial picture of individuals' well-being and therefore are of limited value in understanding the factors behind the Arab Spring.

Notes

1. Studies have shown that the difference between the best and the worst possible health is worth millions of dollars per year (that is, more income than is available) (Clark, Frijters, and Shields 2008). A job is also estimated to be worth about twice mean yearly income, according to estimates by Carroll, Frijters, and Shields (2009) for Australia.
2. Frijters, Shields, and Haisken-DeNew (2002), for example, find that in 1991 people in East Germany did not fully anticipate that their initial euphoria over German reunification would wear off and overestimated their future life satisfaction.
3. Veenhoven (2000) discusses the differences in the meanings of the terms quality of life, well-being, and happiness in depth.
4. The World Happiness Report also relies on Cantril Scale measures of subjective well-being.
5. Because there is uncertainty about to what degree index makers' opinions matter, it is hard to treat an index as an overall measure of well-being or to assess the extent to which variations in individual components affect overall scores. Several indexes provide global coverage, including the United Nations Development Programme's Human Development Index, the Happy Planet Index, the Legatum Prosperity Index, and the Gallup-Healthways Well-Being Index. Other indexes are country-specific well-being indexes prepared for Bhutan, Canada, Italy, the United States, or groups of countries such as those in the Organisation for Economic Co-operation and Development. Each of these indexes serves a specific purpose, but none is a direct measure of subjective well-being, although some rely on subjective well-being measures for a small part of the overall index, for picking components that are in line with life evaluations, or for weights on the well-being part of their prosperity index. In addition, these indexes conflate conditions for and outcomes of well-being.
6. Population-based samples in each country enable cross-country comparisons.

7. The World Values Survey and Arab Barometer surveys are two other sources of information, but they do not offer information on an annual basis for each Arab country.
8. In 2009, Libya was an exception.

References

Arampatzi, E., M. Burger, E. Ianchovichina, T. Röhricht, and R. Veenhoven. 2015. "Unhappy Development: Dissatisfaction with Life on the Eve of the Arab Spring." Policy Research Working Paper 7488, World Bank, Washington, DC.

Bertrand, M., and S. Mullainathan. 2001. "Do People Mean What They Say? Implications for Subjective Survey Data." *American Economic Review* 91: 67–72.

Cantril, H. 1965. *The Pattern of Human Concerns*. New Brunswick, NJ: Rutgers University Press.

Carroll, N., P. Frijters, and M. A. Shields. 2009. "Quantifying the Costs of Drought: New Evidence from Life Satisfaction Data." *Journal of Population Economics* 22 (2): 445–61.

Clark, A. E., P. Frijters, and M. A. Shields. 2008. "Relative Income, Happiness, and Utility: An Explanation for the Easterlin Paradox and Other Puzzles." *Journal of Economic Literature* 46: 95–144.

Deaton, A. 2008. "Income, Health and Well-Being around the World: Evidence from the Gallup World Poll." *Journal of Economic Perspectives* 22: 53–72.

Deci, E., and R. Ryan. 2000. "The 'What' and 'Why' of Goal Pursuits: Human Needs and the Self-Determination of Behaviour." *Psychological Inquiry* 11: 227–68.

Diener, E., D. Kahneman, R. Arora, J. Harter, and W. Tov. 2009. "Income's Differential Influence on Judgments of Life Versus Affective Well-Being." In *Assessing Well-Being: The Collected Works of Ed Diener*, edited by E. Diener. Social Indicators Research Series 39. Berlin: Springer Science and Business Media.

Femia, F., and C. Werrell. 2012. "Syria: Climate Change, Drought and Social Unrest." The Center for Climate and Security, February 29.

Frijters, P., M. A. Shields, and J. P. Haisken-DeNew. 2002. "Individual Rationality and Learning: Welfare Expectations in East Germany Post-Reunification." IZA Discussion Paper 498, Institute for the Study of Labor, Bonn.

Kahneman, D., E. Diener, and N. Schwarz, eds. 1999. *Foundations of Hedonic Psychology: Scientific Perspectives on Enjoyment and Suffering*. New York: Russell Sage Foundation.

Kahneman, D., P. Wakker, and R. Sarin. 1997. "Back to Bentham: Explorations of Experienced Utility." *Quarterly Journal of Economics* 112: 375–405.

Kimball, M., and R. Willis. 2006. "Utility and Happiness." Unpublished, University of Michigan.

Layard, R. 2006. *Happiness. Lessons from a New Science*. London: Allen Lane.

Maslow, A. H. 1943. "A Theory of Human Motivation." *Psychological Review* 50: 370–96.

Rabin, M. 1998. "Psychology and Economics." *Journal of Economic Literature* 36: 11–46.

Ryff, C. 1989. "Happiness Is Everything, or Is It? Explorations on the Meaning of Psychological Well-Being." *Journal of Personality and Social Psychology* 57: 1069–81.

Ryff, C. and B. Singer. 1998. "The Contours of Positive Human Health." *Psychological Inquiry* 9: 1–28.

Seligman, M. 2002. *Authentic Happiness: Using the New Positive Psychology to Realize Your Potential for Lasting Fulfillment*. New York: Free Press.

Veenhoven, R. 1984. *Conditions of Happiness*. Dordrecht/Boston: Reidel.

———. 2000. "The Four Qualities of Life: Ordering Concepts and Measures of the Good Life." *Journal of Happiness Studies* 1: 1–39.

———. 2012. "Happiness: Also Known As 'Life Satisfaction' and 'Subjective Well-Being.'" In *Handbook of Social Indicators and Quality of Life Research*, edited by K. C. Land, A. C. Michalos, and M. J. Sirgy. Berlin: Springer.

CHAPTER 4

Subjective Well-Being Dynamics

Introduction

The synthetic panel analysis with objective expenditure data, presented in chapter 2, provides some evidence on the middle class squeeze in developing Arab countries. However, the full extent of the squeeze on the middle class becomes apparent only after undertaking synthetic panel analysis with subjective well-being data. This analysis reveals significant increases in the ranks of dissatisfied and struggling people and a decline in the ranks of satisfied people[1] in each Arab Spring country in the period immediately preceding the Arab Spring (figure 4.1, panel a).[2] Dissatisfaction rates increased in some other developing Arab countries too (figure 4.1, panel b). These increases were largest in the Arab Republic of Egypt, Morocco, and the Syrian Arab Republic, where between 10 and 20 percent of the population (ages 15 to 55) became dissatisfied with their lives between 2007 and 2010. At the end of the first decade of the 2000s, the Middle East and North Africa (MENA) was the only region in the world with a high incidence of steep declines in subjective well-being (map 4.1). The declines were more pronounced, on average, among the top 60 percent than the bottom 40 percent of the surveyed population (map 4.2), especially in the Arab Spring countries—Egypt, Libya, Syria, Tunisia, and the Republic of Yemen. This result suggests that the Arab Spring events appear to have been precipitated by broadly shared concerns that negatively affected the well-being of the middle classes.

Objective and Subjective Well-Being: Mixed Evidence

Before the Arab Spring, both poverty and dissatisfaction rates were rising in Egypt and the Republic of Yemen (see table 2.3 and figure 4.1,

FIGURE 4.1

Dissatisfaction Rates, by Country, 2007–12

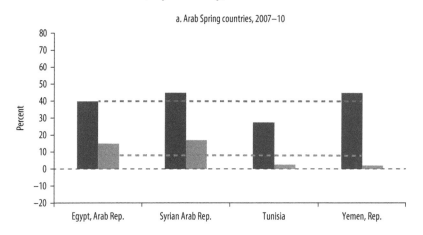

a. Arab Spring countries, 2007–10

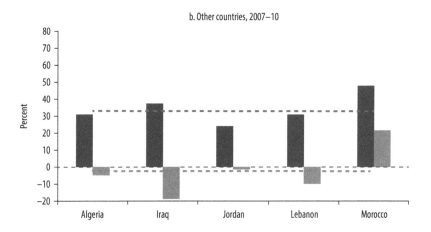

b. Other countries, 2007–10

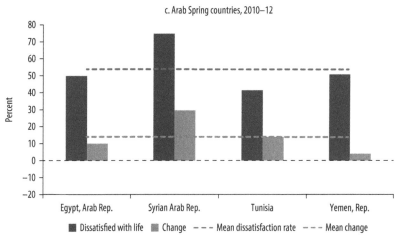

c. Arab Spring countries, 2010–12

■ Dissatisfied with life ■ Change – – – Mean dissatisfaction rate – – – Mean change

(continued on next page)

FIGURE 4.1

Dissatisfaction Rates, by Country, 2007–12 *Continued*

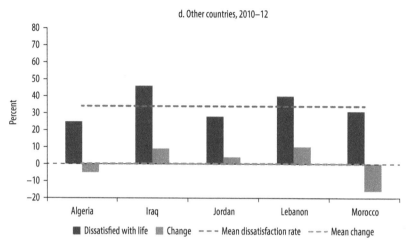

d. Other countries, 2010–12

■ Dissatisfied with life ■ Change – – – Mean dissatisfaction rate – – – Mean change

Source: Dang and Ianchovichina 2016.
Note: The unhappy are those ages 15 to 55 with life satisfaction scores of 4 and below.

MAP 4.1

Changes in Subjective Well-Being, 2009–10

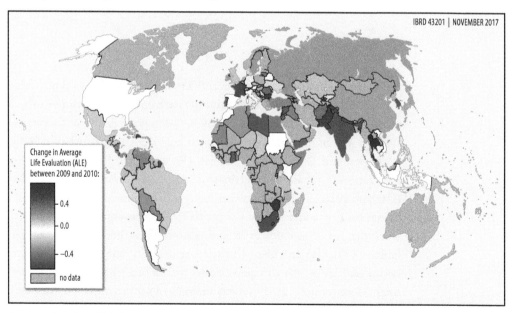

IBRD 43201 | NOVEMBER 2017

Change in Average
Life Evaluation (ALE)
between 2009 and 2010:

0.4

0.0

−0.4

no data

Source: Data from Gallup World Poll.
Note: The map illustrates absolute changes in average life satisfaction scores by country between 2009 and 2010.

MAP 4.2

Subjective Well-Being Change, Top 60 Percent to Bottom 40 Percent, 2009–10

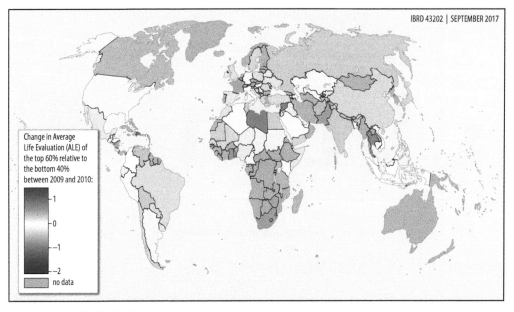

Source: Data from Gallup World Poll.
Note: The map illustrates absolute change in average life evaluation of the top 60 percent between 2009 and 2010 minus the absolute change in average life evaluation of the bottom 40 percent between 2009 and 2010, by country.

respectively), but poverty in Syria and Tunisia was falling at a time of rising dissatisfaction rates. These findings are consistent with the mixed evidence in the literature on the link between poverty and unhappiness. Poverty and unhappiness are found to not necessarily overlap in India (Banerjee and Duflo 2007), Mexico (Rojas 2008), Peru, the Russian Federation (Graham and Pettinato 2002), and various other countries (Graham 2010). The link between changes in income and subjective well-being was first addressed by Easterlin (1974), who argues in his seminal work that, as economies grow and nations get richer, they do not get happier.[3] He also provides evidence that in the developed world, where basic needs are satisfied, richer societies are not much happier than poorer ones. More recently, attention has shifted to a pattern observed in several transition countries, where high economic growth was accompanied by declining levels of well-being within countries (for example, Brockmann et al. 2009; Easterlin et al. 2012; Graham, Zhou, and Zhang 2015). Controlling for per capita income, several cross-country studies by Deaton (2008), Graham and Lora (2009), and Stevenson and

Wolfers (2008) even find that people living in fast-growing economies are, on average, less happy than those living in slow-growing economies. This phenomenon, referred to by Graham and Lora (2009) as the "unhappy growth" paradox, highlights the importance of taking into account people's perceptions when attempting to understand a nation's well-being.

The rise in dissatisfaction rates in most Arab countries was surprising in the context of declining poverty rates in nearly all Arab states except Egypt and the Republic of Yemen (table 2.3) and improvements in many development indicators, including improved access to infrastructure and health and education services and reduced child and maternal mortality throughout the MENA region (Iqbal and Kiendrebeogo, forthcoming). In addition, although the size of the middle class increased in some countries according to estimates based on expenditure data (compare table 2.2 and table 2.6), the share of satisfied individuals declined in nearly all Arab countries, with declines being most pronounced in the Arab Spring countries (figure 4.2). Arampatzi et al. (2015) call this decline in the level of subjective well-being at a time of development progress, the "unhappy development" paradox. This study shows that the paradox can more accurately be characterized as the unhappy development syndrome, reflecting the symptoms of a broken social contract.

FIGURE 4.2

Share of Satisfied Individuals in Total Population, 2005–12

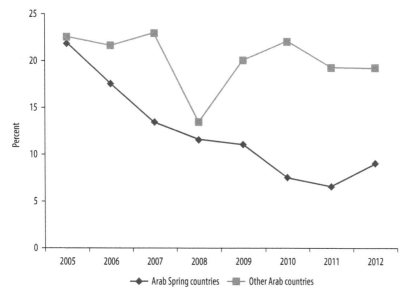

Source: Dang and Ianchovichina 2016.
Note: The satisfied individuals are those with life satisfaction scores of 8 or above.

There are several explanations for the unhappy development syndrome. According to Devarajan and Ianchovichina (2017), the subjective well-being data capture the increased frustration with symptoms of a broken social contract. Access to public services had increased, but over the years the quality of these services had declined, forcing millions of people to stop going to public health clinics and schools and start spending on private services. Under such circumstances, the expenditure-based welfare indicator is biased because increases in per capita expenditure may reflect not only genuine increases in welfare attributable to increased consumption but also the substitution of public for private services and the need to increase private spending to pay for these services by borrowing, depleting savings, or working long hours. Changes in nonmonetary circumstances may also reduce subjective well-being while increasing expenditures. For instance, pollution associated with high energy subsidies may increase health costs and thus the expenditure-based welfare indicators but cause unhappiness because health has been shown to be a major determinant of well-being. Of course, the subjective well-being indicator provides a more complete picture under such circumstances.

With increases in literacy and access to education, people's aspirations might have risen, particularly those of young people who were better educated than their parents and hoped to find good jobs after graduation but ended up struggling to make ends meet (Campante and Chor 2012; Devarajan and Ianchovichina 2017). As they failed to meet their aspirations, people's aversion to social injustice, corruption, and inequality grew along with their anger and unhappiness (Cammett and Diwan 2013). According to Graham and Pettinato (2002), economic growth that is not broadly shared may result in a middle class consisting of "frustrated achievers." This reasoning is in line with the "tunnel effect," introduced by Hirschman (1973), which occurs in situations similar to traffic congestion in a tunnel where one of the lanes starts moving while the other ones are still jammed. Those who are still stuck initially feel hope because the end of the traffic jam seems to be in sight, but after some time, if their lane remains blocked, hope gives way to envy and anger. In response, the people who are stuck may try—perhaps in violation of the law—to change lanes. In the Arab world, the tunnel effect may have been felt by the upper middle class, in particular, given that reforms implemented to boost economic growth mostly benefited the elites with connections to the regimes in power. The next chapter presents evidence that associates the decline in subjective well-being in Arab countries to frustration with the symptoms of a broken social contract, specifically the erosion in the quality of life and widespread corruption.

Subjective Well-Being Dynamics with Synthetic Panels

The analysis of subjective well-being dynamics with synthetic panels[4] provides some evidence of the intensity of social upheaval, proxied by the change in the percentage of dissatisfied individuals in Arab countries during the transition period spanning the Arab Spring.[5] Following the 2013 Gallup World Poll the unhappy (or dissatisfied) group is defined as those with life evaluation scores of 4 and below. Given this dissatisfaction threshold for subjective well-being, the vulnerability line is specified in a similar way to the vulnerability approach adopted for the objective welfare measure and discussed in chapter 2. However, because the subjective welfare measure is a discrete variable with only 10 values, there are only a few usable values for the vulnerability line above the "poverty" line of 4. Dang and Ianchovichina (2016) choose a vulnerability index of 30 percent, which lies roughly in the mid-range of the possible vulnerability indexes and yields a mid-range vulnerability line of 7. The struggling group is then composed of those with life evaluation scores between 5 and 7, and the happy (or satisfied) are those with well-being scores of 8 or above.[6]

The growth patterns for the different satisfaction categories suggest that many struggling and satisfied people became dissatisfied (table 4.1). In the developing Arab countries as a whole, during the period between 2009 and 2012 the average dissatisfaction rate increased and subjective well-being declined for the average individual (table 4.1, last row).

TABLE 4.1

Change in the Size of Subjective Well-Being Categories, 2009–12

percent

Country	Dissatisfied	Struggling	Satisfied	Annual growth in mean satisfaction
Morocco	−26.7	20.1	37.0	1.3
Algeria	12.0	−11.4	34.7	−0.1
Iraq	6.0	−9.5	43.3	−0.3
Lebanon	39.5	−8.6	−43.8	−4.4
Tunisia	74.3	−22.4	−30.9	−5.2
Jordan	91.7	−8.6	−46.3	−5.5
Yemen, Rep.	22.3	−6.4	−49.3	−6.0
Egypt, Arab Rep.	71.1	−28.1	−38.5	−6.4
Syrian Arab Rep.	100.3	−66.3	−38.1	−14.4
Average	43.4	−15.7	−14.7	−4.6

Source: Dang and Ianchovichina 2016.
Note: The categories of subjective well-being are defined as follows: (1) dissatisfied individuals are those with life satisfaction scores of 4 or below; (2) struggling individuals have life satisfaction scores of 5, 6, or 7; and (3) satisfied individuals are those with life satisfaction scores of 8 or above. All estimates are obtained using population weights; regional averages are unweighted simple averages. Respondent's age is between 15 and 55 in the first survey round and adjusted accordingly for the second survey round.

This deteriorating trend was stronger in the Arab Spring countries than elsewhere in the Arab world between 2007 and 2010 (figure 4.1), indicating stronger demand for change in the Arab Spring countries than elsewhere in the MENA region, and between 2009 and 2012, when increases in dissatisfaction rates also reflected the effects of the tumultuous transitions (table 4.2). While the share of dissatisfied individuals in the total

TABLE 4.2

Subjective Well-Being Transition Dynamics with Synthetic Panels

percent

		2012			
A. Arab Spring countries		Dissatisfied	Struggling	Satisfied	Total
2009	Dissatisfied	17.8	10.0	1.5	29.3
		(0.1)	(0.0)	(0.0)	(0.1)
	Struggling	23.8	24.3	6.1	54.2
		(0.0)	(0.0)	(0.0)	(0.0)
	Satisfied	4.7	8.3	3.6	16.5
		(0.0)	(0.0)	(0.0)	(0.0)
	Total	46.3	42.5	11.2	100
		(0.1)	(0.0)	(0.0)	
		2012			
B. Other Arab countries		Dissatisfied	Struggling	Satisfied	Total
2009	Dissatisfied	11.7	5.8	0.3	17.8
		(0.0)	(0.0)	(0.0)	(0.1)
	Struggling	13.3	31.7	8.8	53.7
		(0.0)	(0.0)	(0.0)	(0.0)
	Satisfied	1.1	11.9	15.5	28.4
		(0.0)	(0.0)	(0.1)	(0.1)
	Total	26.0	49.4	24.5	100
		(0.1)	(0.0)	(0.1)	(0.0)
		2012			
C. All Arab countries		Dissatisfied	Struggling	Satisfied	Total
2009	Dissatisfied	15.3	5.9	0.3	21.5
		(0.0)	(0.0)	(0.0)	(0.0)
	Struggling	16.3	30.2	7.5	54.0
		(0.0)	(0.0)	(0.0)	(0.0)
	Satisfied	1.4	11.0	12.2	24.5
		(0.0)	(0.0)	(0.0)	(0.1)
	Total	33.0	47.1	20.0	100
		(0.0)	(0.0)	(0.0)	

Source: Dang and Ianchovichina 2016.
Note: All estimates are obtained using population weights; regional average is unweighted simple average. Respondent's age is between 15 and 55 in the first survey round and adjusted accordingly for the second survey round. Bootstrap standard errors in parentheses are estimated with 1,000 bootstraps. The sample in panel A includes 9,192 individuals from Arab Spring countries (the Arab Republic of Egypt, Libya, the Syrian Arab Republic, Tunisia, and the Republic of Yemen) and in panel B 17,652 individuals from the other Arab countries (Algeria, Bahrain, the Islamic Republic of Iran, Iraq, Jordan, Kuwait, Lebanon, Morocco, Qatar, Saudi Arabia, and the United Arab Emirates).

population of other Arab countries increased by 46 percent,[7] in the Arab Spring countries this share increased by 58 percent. At the same time, the reduction in the shares of struggling and satisfied people was much more pronounced in the Arab Spring countries than elsewhere in the Arab world. By 2012, almost half of the population in the Arab Spring countries was dissatisfied with their lives compared with slightly less than a third in 2009. In other Arab countries, the share of dissatisfied people increased from less than one-fifth (18 percent) of the population in 2009 to slightly more than one-fourth (26 percent) of the population in 2012.[8]

Another useful way to gauge subjective welfare dynamics is to look at the percentage of the population for whom the welfare status changed during this period. Some 21 percent[9] of the population moved up one or two subjective welfare categories in both Arab Spring countries and other Arab countries (table 4.2). However, the percentage of people who moved down one or two welfare categories in the Arab Spring countries is 52 percent, much higher than the corresponding figure of 32 percent in the other Arab countries. The region-wide trend is qualitatively similar, with 18 percent of the population moving up one or two subjective welfare categories and 37 percent moving down one or two subjective welfare categories (table 4.2).

Figure 4.3 displays the percentage of upwardly (downwardly) mobile (those who move up [down] one or two welfare categories)

FIGURE 4.3

Subjective Well-Being Dynamics, by Country, 2009–12

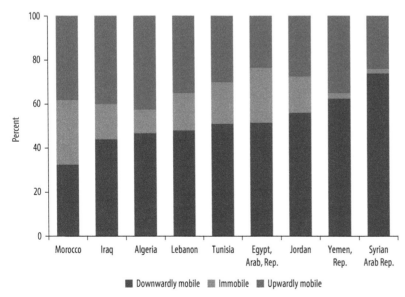

Source: Dang and Ianchovichina 2016.
Note: All estimates are obtained using population weights. Respondent's age is between 15 and 55 in the first survey round and adjusted accordingly for the second survey round.

and the percentage of immobile (those who remain in the same income category) by country. The figure illustrates that, in the context of subjective well-being, there was less upward mobility and more downward mobility in the Arab Spring countries—Egypt, Syria, Tunisia, and the Republic of Yemen—compared with other Arab countries. Downward mobility was much more pronounced for the Arab Spring countries than elsewhere in the Arab world (figure 4.4). In the Arab Spring countries, people without education, those in rural areas, and migrants were considerably more vulnerable to downward mobility than were other groups (figure 4.4). Migrants and the most educated citizens in other Arab countries were considerably less likely to move downward and had better-than-average chances of becoming more satisfied with their lives (figure 4.4). The next chapter examines the factors behind the high rates of dissatisfaction in the Arab countries and links them to the symptoms of a broken social contract.

FIGURE 4.4

Subjective Well-Being Dynamics in Arab Spring Countries and Other Arab Countries, by Population Group, 2007–12

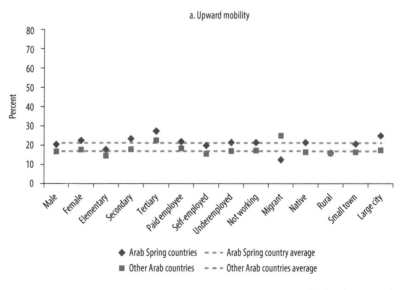

(continued on next page)

FIGURE 4.4

Subjective Well-Being Dynamics in Arab Spring Countries and Other Arab Countries, by Population Group, 2007–12   *Continued*

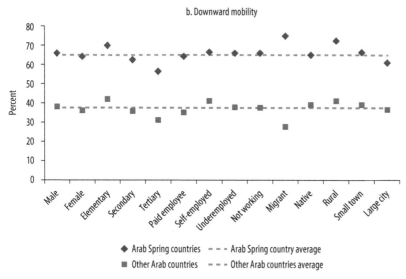

Source: Dang and Ianchovichina 2016.

Notes

1. See chapter 3 for definitions of satisfied, dissatisfied, and struggling people.
2. Figure 4.1 shows dissatisfaction rates for a sample restricted to ages 15 to 55. The rate of dissatisfaction among these surveyed individuals up to age 55 is significantly higher than for the general sample, reflecting the greater dissatisfaction among the young generations.
3. For a critique of this viewpoint, see Hagerty and Veenhoven (2003) and Stevenson and Wolfers (2008). For further discussion, see Clark, Frijters, and Shields (2008).
4. The analysis is based on subjective well-being regressions estimated by Dang and Ianchovichina (2016).
5. Witte, Burger, and Ianchovichina (2017) find that a decrease in average subjective well-being—and particularly an increase in self-reported suffering—leads to an increase in nonviolent uprisings.
6. An alternative would be to use a vulnerability line of 6, which roughly corresponds to an index of vulnerability similar to the one used in the objective well-being analysis presented in chapter 2. Dang and Ianchovichina (2016) present estimation results based on this alternative specification for the vulnerability line, and these results are similar to the ones presented in this chapter.
7. Please note that 46 percent is derived as (26/17.8) – 1.
8. Qualitatively similar results are offered by estimations using somewhat different thresholds for the dissatisfied and struggling groups, resulting in definitions of satisfied, dissatisfied, and struggling people as in chapter 3 (that is, defining the individuals who are dissatisfied and struggling as those with satisfaction scores of 5 and below and between 6 and 7, respectively) and an

alternative specification using the 40th and 80th percentiles to define the groups of dissatisfied and struggling. These results are provided in Dang and Ianchovichina (2016).

9. Please note that 21 percent is derived as $(10 + 1.5 + 6.1)/(29.3 + 54.2)$.

References

Arampatzi, E., M. Burger, E. Ianchovichina, T. Rohricht, and R. Veenhoven. 2015. "Unhappy Development: Dissatisfaction with Life on the Eve of the Arab Spring." Policy Research Working Paper 7488, World Bank, Washington, DC.

Banerjee, A., and E. Duflo. 2007. "The Economic Lives of the Poor." *Journal of Economic Perspectives* 21 (1): 141–67.

Brockmann, H., J. Delhey, C. Welzeland, and H. Yuan. 2009. "The China Puzzle: Falling Happiness in a Rising Economy." *Journal of Happiness Studies* 10: 387–405.

Campante, F. R., and D. Chor. 2012. "Why Was the Arab World Poised for Revolution? Schooling, Economic Opportunities, and the Arab Spring." *Journal of Economic Perspectives* 26: 167–88.

Cammett, M. C., and I. Diwan. 2013. *The Political Economy of the Arab Uprisings.* New York: Perseus Books Group.

Clark, A. E., P. Frijters, and M. A. Shields. 2008. "Relative Income, Happiness, and Utility: An Explanation for the Easterlin Paradox and Other Puzzles." *Journal of Economic Literature* 46: 95–144.

Dang, H., and E. Ianchovichina. 2016. "Welfare Dynamics with Synthetic Panels: The Case of the Arab World in Transition." Policy Research Working Paper 7595, World Bank, Washington, DC.

Deaton, A. 2008. "Income, Health and Well-Being around the World: Evidence from the Gallup World Poll." *Journal of Economic Perspectives* 22: 53–72.

Devarajan, S., and E. Ianchovichina. 2017. "A Broken Social Contract, Not High Inequality, Led to the Arab Spring." *Review of Income and Wealth*, published online.

Dresch, P. 2000. *History of Modern Yemen.* Cambridge, UK: Cambridge University Press.

Easterlin, R. 1974. "Does Economic Growth Improve the Human Lot? Some Empirical Evidence." In *Nations and Households in Economic Growth: Essays in Honor of Moses Abramovitz,* edited by R. David and R. Reder. New York: Academic Press.

Easterlin, R., R. Morgan, M. Switekand, and F. Wang. 2012. "China's Life Satisfaction, 1990–2010." *Proceedings of the National Academy of Sciences* 109 (25): 9775–80.

Graham, C. 2010. *Happiness around the World: The Paradox of Happy Peasants and Miserable Millionaires.* New York: Oxford University Press.

Graham, C., and E. Lora. 2009. "Happiness and Health Satisfaction across Countries." In *Paradox and Perception: Measuring Quality of Life in Latin America,* edited by C. Graham and E. Lora. Washington, DC: Brookings Institution Press.

Graham, C., and S. Pettinato. 2002. "Frustrated Achievers: Winners, Losers and Subjective Well-Being in New Market Economies." *Journal of Development Studies* 38 (4): 100–40.

Graham, C., S. Zhou, and J. Zhang. 2015. "Happiness and Health in China: The Paradox of Progress." Global Economy & Development at Brookings, Working Paper 89, Brookings Institution, Washington, DC.

Hagerty, M. R., and R. Veenhoven. 2003. "Wealth and Happiness Revisited— Growing National Income Does Go with Greater Happiness." *Social Indicators Research* 64: 1–27.

Hirschman, A. O. 1973. "The Changing Tolerance for Income Inequality in the Course of Economic Development, with a Mathematical Appendix by Michael Rothschild." *Quarterly Journal of Economics* 87 (4): 544–66.

Iqbal, F., and Y. Kiendrebeogo. Forthcoming. "The Determinants of Child Mortality Reduction in the Middle East and North Africa." *Middle East Development Journal*.

Rojas, M. 2008. "Experienced Poverty and Income Poverty in Mexico: A Subjective Well-Being Approach." *World Development* 36 (6): 1078–93.

Stevenson, B., and J. Wolfers. 2008. "Economic Growth and Subjective Well-Being: Reassessing the Easterlin Paradox." *Brookings Papers on Economic Activity* 2008 (Spring): 1–87.

Witte, C., M. Burger, and E. Ianchovichina. 2017. "Unhappy Rebels: The Role of Subjective Well-Being in Civil Conflict." Unpublished.

Symptoms of a Broken Social Contract

Introduction

A look at the universal conditions for happiness, as presented in cross-country studies focusing on life satisfaction, provides limited understanding of the root causes of dissatisfaction with life in the Arab world. To understand the factors shaping subjective well-being in the developing Arab countries before the Arab Spring, the social context in these countries during this period must be explicitly factored in. This chapter does so by considering several explanations proffered for the eruption of popular Arab anger in 2011, including (1) limited freedom and voice in predominantly autocratic states, (2) dissatisfaction with standards of living, (3) unhappiness with persistent unemployment and lack of good jobs caused by the growing informality of the private sector, and (4) dissatisfaction with corruption and cronyism, which limits opportunities for those who work hard. Each of these explanations is also a symptom of the broken social contract in place before the Arab Spring.

A Broken Social Contract

To understand why people were dissatisfied with the quality of their lives despite improvements in objective economic and development indicators, this section discusses the social contract and notes that all countries in the Middle East and North Africa (MENA) region had had more or less the same social contract since independence, and in many developing countries the social contracts were kept in place through coercion.[1] One of the main features of the contract was the dominant role of the central government, which was the main employer. As a result, the public sector dominated formal sector employment (figure 5.1). The state provided free education and health, and subsidized food and fuel, with fuel expenditures often accounting for a significant portion of public spending (figure 5.2). In return for the state's assistance, citizens were expected to keep their voices low, and government's accountability to citizens was weak (figure 5.3). Power was concentrated in the hands of one person or a small group of elites, backed by the military, who made

FIGURE 5.1

Distribution of Employment

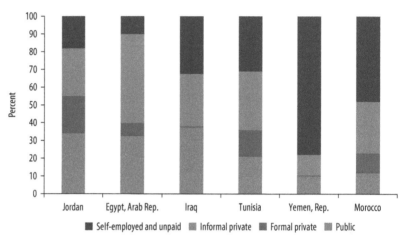

Source: Gatti et al. 2013.

FIGURE 5.2

Allocation of Public Expenditures

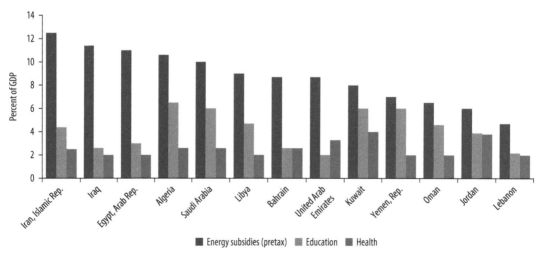

Source: IMF 2014, based on Clements et al. 2013.
Note: GDP = gross domestic product.

FIGURE 5.3

Voice and Accountability and GDP per Capita, 2010

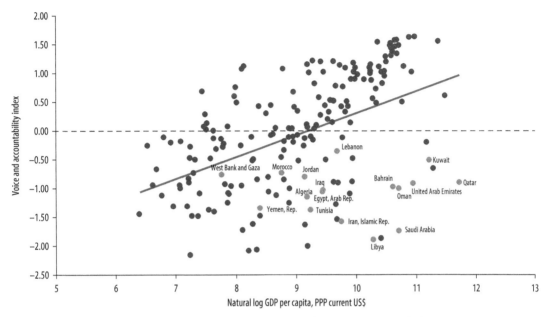

Sources: World Governance Indicators for Voice and Accountability; World Bank, World Development Indicators for GDP per capita.
Note: The voice and accountability index reflects perceptions of the extent to which citizens are able to participate in selecting their government as well as freedom of expression, freedom of association, and a free media. The index ranges from approximately –2.5 for weak to 2.5 for strong estimated performance. GDP = gross domestic product; PPP = purchasing power parity.

decisions subject to few legal restraints and mechanisms of popular control. At the same time, the public had few if any channels through which to safely express opinions and grievances and limited opportunities to develop strong civil society (Chekir and Diwan 2012; Bromley 2014; Cammett and Diwan 2013). Exclusion generated anger about "relative deprivation" between those with connections to elites and those without connections.

This social contract, referred to also as an "autocratic bargain" by Cammett and Diwan (2013), lured the middle class with material benefits in exchange for political quiescence, and it delivered development results. The food subsidies, although expensive and poorly targeted, did keep the poor fed. The public sector worker's salary also served as a safety net for a large number of family members. Access to education and health improved faster than anywhere else in the developing world (Iqbal and Kiendrebeogo, forthcoming). As a result, poverty rates fell, with the regional average extreme poverty rate—the percentage of people living on less than $1.25 a day—reaching 2 percent by 2010, the year of the Arab Spring (figure O.3).

However, starting in the 2000s, it also became clear that this social contract was not sustainable. In particular, the fiscal deficits associated with public sector employment and high subsidies were becoming unsustainable. Government hiring slowed down and, in some cases, stopped. Unfortunately, the private sector was weak and did not create jobs fast enough to absorb the large number of young people entering the labor force. MENA had the highest unemployment rate in the developing world, with the rate for young people and women about double the average (figure 5.4).

Furthermore, the unemployment rate was higher among educated people, presumably because they had sources of support to enable them to "queue" for the scarce but lucrative public sector jobs. Meanwhile, those without these sources of support found work in the informal sector—at very low wages, without the security and protections of formal sector jobs. Many women, not wanting to work in these threatening settings, dropped out of the labor force entirely, resulting in the lowest female labor force participation rate in the world (figure 5.5).

Why, when the public sector was cutting back, did the private sector in MENA not grow and create jobs? A closer look at some countries, such as Tunisia (figure 5.6), reveals a pattern that may be representative of the whole region. Almost all the jobs created were in young, one-person firms, also known as startups (World Bank 2014). The problem was that

FIGURE 5.4

Unemployment Rates

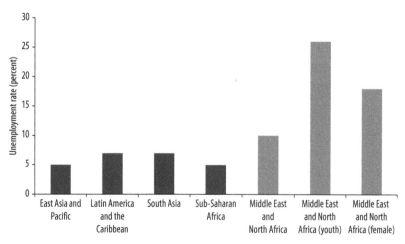

Source: World Bank, World Development Indicators 2014.

FIGURE 5.5

Female Labor Force Participation Rates

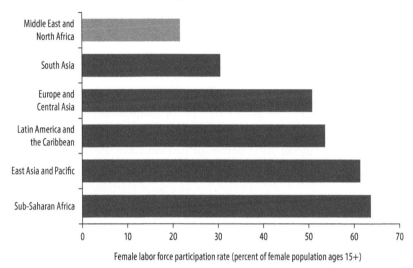

Female labor force participation rate (percent of female population ages 15+)

Source: World Bank, World Development Indicators 2014.

FIGURE 5.6

Net Job Creation in Tunisia, 1996–2010

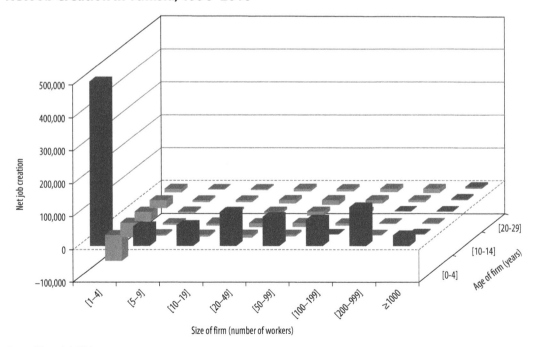

Source: Rijkers et al. 2014.

TABLE 5.1

Evidence of Elite Capture in Tunisia: Ben Ali Family's Share
percent of respective total for Tunisia in 2010

Wage workers	Output	Net profits	Gross profits	Firms
1.7	5.3	15.8	10.8	0.2

Source: Rijkers, Freund, and Nucifora 2017.

these startups hardly ever grew into small or medium-sized firms, which are typically the engines of job creation. Even 10 years later, 95 percent of startups were either still startups or had closed down and exited the market.

Perhaps the most frustrating issue is why these startups never grew. In both Tunisia and the Arab Republic of Egypt, considerable evidence indicates that old, large firms with monopoly power stood in the way of small-enterprise growth. In Egypt, every time a connected firm entered a sector, that sector's rate of job creation fell by 1.4 percent (Schiffbauer et al. 2015). And the reason these firms enjoyed monopoly power was that they were connected with the political elites (Rijkers, Freund, and Nucifora 2017; Schiffbauer et al. 2015). For instance, in Tunisia, former President Ben Ali's family had interests in the banking, telecommunications, and transport sectors (Rijkers, Freund, and Nucifora 2017). While they accounted for less than 2 percent of the total number of workers receiving wages and 5.3 percent of output, the "Ben Ali firms" represented 15.8 percent of net profits in the economy (table 5.1). Connected firms were protected from competition by regulations that prohibited foreign investment and benefited from energy subsidies that biased production in favor of capital-intensive activities. The services sectors remained closed to competition (Hoekman and Sekkat 2009), and the high prices and poor quality of domestic services made it very difficult for small firms—all of which need banking, telecommunications, and transport inputs—to compete in world markets. Uncompetitive currencies (Freund and Jaud 2015), political instability (Burger, Ianchovichina, and Rijkers 2016), and inequitable distribution of resource rents (Behzadan et al. 2017) created Dutch disease dynamics, hurting the tradables sectors in many MENA countries. Under the protection of regulations, large domestic companies had no incentives to invest to compete, expand market share, or innovate. In short, crony capitalism and a host of distortions stood in the way of private sector job creation in Tunisia and other developing MENA countries. These findings about the lack of dynamism in the private sector help explain why the more affluent and educated middle-class citizens, who were seeking formal sector jobs, were the most dissatisfied with the standards of living in their countries.

In addition to failing on the jobs front, the old social contract was unraveling in a second dimension. Although health and education were provided for free, and energy and water consumption were subsidized, the quality of these public services was so poor that people ended up paying the private sector to obtain them. For instance, although school enrollment rates were almost universal, learning outcomes were disappointing. On internationally comparable standardized tests, children in MENA performed significantly worse than students from much poorer countries (figure 5.7). One reason is that teacher absenteeism rates in public schools in MENA were among the highest in the world (Brixi, Lust, and Woolcock 2015). Because teachers were paid regardless of whether they showed up in the classroom, many chose to tutor students privately or work elsewhere. Similarly, doctors in public clinics in Egypt were found to be absent 32 percent of the time; the comparable figures for Morocco and the Republic of Yemen were 27 percent and 37 percent, respectively. Seeking quality education and health care, people were sending their children for private tutoring (the proportion of students receiving tutoring in Egypt was 70 percent) in the pre–Arab Spring period, and going to fee-paying private clinics for health care. As one woman in Egypt put it, "A public hospital is where you lose your life…a private one is where you lose your money…" (World Bank 2013, 35).

FIGURE 5.7

Learning Outcomes: PISA Math Scores in Relation to GDP per Capita

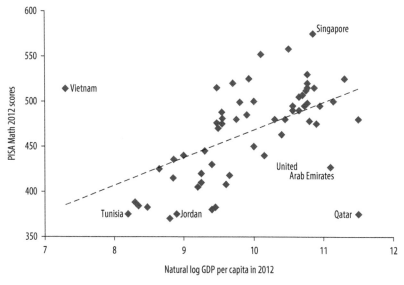

Source: PISA Math 2012.
Note: GDP = gross domestic product; PISA = Programme for International Student Assessment.

The increase in private spending on services sent a misleading signal that welfare was improving when, in fact, people were frustrated and growing less happy. In many instances, individuals had to cover the increases in expenditures on education and health services either by borrowing, depleting their savings, or working longer hours.

Likewise, the web of fuel and energy subsidies led to underspending on infrastructure maintenance, which, in turn, meant that energy services were of poor quality. In fact, the MENA region had, on average, the highest incidence of electricity cutoffs in the world (Devarajan and Mottaghi 2014). In addition, diesel fuel subsidies gave farmers an incentive to use water pumps to such an extent that MENA became the most water-scarce region in the world. Of course, plenty of evidence also suggests that these subsidies benefited the rich far more than they did the poor, while crowding out spending on genuine public goods.

In short, the frustration with the lack of formal sector jobs and the poor quality of public services provided evidence of the government's failure to keep its side of the social contract. Because exclusion was a problem and the social contracts in many developing Arab countries were kept in place through coercion, their breakdown increased the premium on freedom and created impetus for political and economic change.

Major Grievances behind the Arab Unhappiness

Systematic analysis of the relative importance of factors influencing subjective well-being in developing Arab countries can be found in Arampatzi et al. (2015). Using data from the Gallup World Poll for 2009 and 2010 and a reduced-form life satisfaction model, Arampatzi et al. (2015) empirically test the direction and strength of the associations between the symptoms of the broken social contract and subjective well-being, while also incorporating objective conditions such as gender; age; marital, financial, health, and education status; and country and time fixed effects (Di Tella, MacCulloch, and Oswald 2003; Arampatzi et al. 2015). A rise in people's expectations and aspirations, particularly those of youth who had acquired better education than their parents and expected to find good jobs after graduation (Campante and Chor 2012) may have also played a role and may have widened the gap between actual and expected well-being. This, in turn, may have increased people's aversion to inequality and social injustice (Verme et al. 2014; Cammett and Diwan 2013), and it may have negatively affected their levels of happiness. According to Graham and Pettinato (2002), the economic growth in Arab countries may have been accompanied by the rise of a middle class consisting of "frustrated achievers," a reasoning in line with Hirschman's (1973) "tunnel effect." The life satisfaction variable indirectly captures the effect of a gap between expectations and reality, but the fact that it does so indirectly makes it difficult to disentangle the effect of expectations from the effect of other subjective and objective factors.

Among the main subjective factors (or symptoms of the broken social contract) investigated by Arampatzi et al. (2015) are those related to the domain-specific characteristics thought to have had the strongest influence on life satisfaction on the eve of the Arab Spring: (1) limited freedom (a concept related to lack of inclusion), (2) eroded standards of living, (3) poor labor market conditions, and (4) governance issues.

Limited Freedom

Because most Arab states were long-standing autocracies (Chekir and Diwan 2012; Bromley 2014; Cammett and Diwan 2013), examining the effect of limited personal freedoms on subjective well-being is important. Arampatzi et al. (2015) do so by including responses to questions on personal freedom, specifically, "Are you satisfied or dissatisfied with your freedom to choose what you do with your life?" The literature has produced mixed results on the link between personal freedom and happiness. Some studies find that the extent to which people are free to make choices and voice opinions has a major impact on their happiness (Inglehart et al. 2008; Verme 2009). People in democracies are, on average, happier than people in autocracies (Frey and Stutzer 2000), and the effect of democracy on happiness is stronger in countries with established democratic traditions (Dorn et al. 2007). But other studies find no significant relationship between voice and accountability and happiness in developing MENA countries (Fereidouni, Najdi, and Amiri 2013) and only a weak correlation between happiness and democracy in the MENA region (Ott 2010). As argued in Arampatzi et al. (2015), the "autocratic bargain" may have weakened the direct link between happiness and limited freedom in developing Arab countries. Individuals who obtain material benefits in exchange for political support may initially express dissatisfaction with living conditions rather than with the system responsible for their deterioration. However, as material benefits erode, the premium on freedom increases, creating impetus not only for economic but also for political change.

Eroded Standards of Living

The failure to deliver quality public services and public sector jobs affected people's standards of living in the developing MENA countries. By the end of the first decade of the 2000s, this erosion in standards of living was felt not only by the poor but also by other segments of the population, including the middle class. Reflecting diminishing marginal utility, the widespread system of subsidies could not compensate for the erosion of living standards; food and energy subsidies mattered less for the well-being of the middle class than they did for the well-being of the poor and vulnerable (Ianchovichina, Mottaghi, and Devarajan 2015). A gradual shift in government support to the elites became a particular concern (Cammett and Diwan 2013). People were frustrated because they could not get ahead by working hard and share in the prosperity generated by the few large Arab firms, which were mostly state-owned or privately owned companies (OECD 2009).

Arampatzi et al. (2015) capture the erosion in living standards by including individual income (expressed in international dollars) and subjective evaluations of living standards based on responses to the following question: "Are you satisfied or dissatisfied with your standard of living, all the things you can buy and do?" The answers to this question reflect how people value both monetary and nonmonetary factors affecting their standards of living, including those related to local institutions, access to infrastructure, health and education services, community safety and cohesion, political and economic stability, as well as those related to the quality of jobs, the environment, the variety of choices available to people living in a given area, and the cultural context. The answers to this question factor in people's own views on what their standards of living should be, given the amount of effort they spend at work and their past expectations. In addition, Arampatzi et al. (2015) include responses to the question, "In the city or area where you live are you satisfied or dissatisfied with the education system or the schools?" The answers capture how people value service provision, in particular education services, which determine employment opportunities later in life.

Poor Labor Market Conditions

The negative association between happiness and unemployment is well established in the literature and can be explained by a combination of income loss and psychic costs related to psychological distress and loss of identity and self-respect (Veenhoven 1989; Gallie and Russell 1998). The detrimental effect of unemployment on happiness has been found to be more severe for the long-term unemployed (Clark and Oswald 1994) and for people with limited job opportunities (Clark, Knabe, and Rätzel 2010).

Dissatisfaction with job market conditions was strong in developing MENA in the pre–Arab Spring period. Employment in the informal sector offered little protection at old age and limited access to quality health care and benefits, such as paid maternity and annual leave (Angel-Urdinola and Kuddo 2011). The mismatch between educational attainment and economic opportunities created a gap between reality and expectations, lowering youth's life satisfaction, amplifying perceptions of unfairness, and potentially contributing to social unrest (Campante and Chor 2012).

In view of the MENA region's persistently high unemployment rates, especially for youth, Arampatzi et al. (2015) include both subjective and objective variables related to employment and the education system. With regard to employment status, they distinguish between individuals who are paid employees (reference category), self-employed, underemployed, unemployed, or out of the workforce.[2] In addition, they factor in whether people are employed in government positions or not (reference category is "Other"), and they reflect on job market conditions and the availability of high-quality jobs by including responses to the question, "Are you satisfied or dissatisfied with efforts to increase the number of quality jobs?"

Governance Issues

Perceptions about corruption and crony capitalism were deteriorating before the Arab Spring (Cammett and Diwan 2013), as reflected in the retreat of MENA countries' rankings on Transparency International's Corruption Perceptions Index between 2000 and 2010. During this period, Tunisia's score declined from 5.2 to 4.3 (lower scores indicate more highly corrupt countries) and Morocco's score decreased from 4.7 to 3.4. In the Syrian Arab Republic, the index dropped from 3.4 in 2003 to 2.5 in 2010. In some countries, including Egypt, Jordan, and Libya, the index was stable, but most MENA countries scored below the worldwide average on various governance indicator rankings in the 2000s (for example, Kaufmann, Kraay, and Mastruzzi 2011).

Private sector growth was stifled by cronyism and fears that a rise of the *nouveau riche* class might challenge existing power relations.[3] Reforms in the 1990s were implemented unevenly, benefiting mainly the elites (Chekir and Diwan 2012; Rijkers, Freund, and Nucifora 2017), who dominated a range of economic sectors (Malik and Awadallah 2013). Corruption and cronyism flourished in developing MENA, with detrimental effects not only on aggregate economic and private sector growth, but also on people's subjective well-being (Ott 2010). Frustration with inequality of opportunity in labor markets and the increased importance of *wasta*, or connections with the elites, in getting good-quality jobs was growing. These feelings were broadly shared and reflected the perceptions of citizens that wasta mattered more than credentials for getting good jobs.

Arampatzi et al. (2015) explore the effect of corruption, cronyism, and wasta on life satisfaction by focusing on perceived government corruption as a proxy for perceptions of corruption in the public and private sectors. They do so by including responses to the question, "Is corruption widespread within government?" and, whenever information regarding corruption in government was not available, responses to the question "Is corruption widespread within business?" (Helliwell, Layard, and Sachs 2015). In addition, to reflect the extent to which cronyism and inequities affect people's life satisfaction, they incorporate people's opinions on whether working hard pays off.

Relative Importance of Major Grievances

The results of Arampatzi et al. (2015) suggest that, among all these factors, dissatisfaction with standards of living has had the biggest negative effect on the level of life satisfaction in MENA, followed by dissatisfaction with poor labor market conditions and perceptions of inequality of opportunities (or wasta) and corruption (figure 5.8). On average,

FIGURE 5.8

Effects of Different Domains on Life Satisfaction in Developing MENA

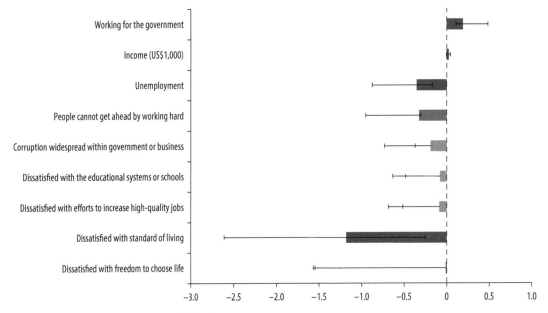

Source: Lewbel (2012) estimates in Arampatzi et al. (2015).
Note: Red, blue, and yellow denote 1 percent significance level, 5 percent significance level, and no significance, respectively. Developing Middle East and North Africa (MENA) includes Algeria, the Arab Republic of Egypt, Iraq, Jordan, Lebanon, Morocco, the Syrian Arab Republic, Tunisia, the West Bank and Gaza, and the Republic of Yemen.

the life satisfaction score of dissatisfied respondents is estimated to be 1.24 points lower than the life satisfaction score of respondents who are satisfied with their living standards. Although dissatisfaction with freedom to make choices has a significant, negative effect on life satisfaction, this effect disappears after controlling for other perceptions (figure 5.8). This finding supports the view that the social contract has weakened the direct link between authoritarianism (for example, lack of freedom) and life satisfaction. People who obtain economic benefits in exchange for political support initially express dissatisfaction not with their limited freedom but with other domains, particularly their economic well-being. However, as material benefits erode, the motivation to demand political change also rises. Dissatisfaction with the efforts of the government to improve the number of high-quality jobs and the educational system do not have a significant effect on life satisfaction. It is likely that these domains are jointly determined or are partly reflected in dissatisfaction with standards of living. However, results suggest that the unemployed are significantly less happy than the employed, and those employed by the government are significantly happier than those working in the private sector. The latter finding is consistent with the fact that public sector jobs often offer higher wages and more job security than do private sector jobs, along with generous social security coverage (Bodor, Robalino, and Rutkowski 2008).

Perceptions of wasta and corruption are significantly and negatively associated with life satisfaction in developing MENA. Respondents who think that people cannot get ahead by working hard report, on average, a 0.22 point lower life satisfaction score than those who are satisfied with this dimension of life satisfaction. This result is consistent with the findings in Rijkers, Freund, and Nucifora (2017) and World Bank (2014) on the effect of cronyism in the private sector.[4] Respondents who believe that corruption in the public sector is widespread are, on average, 0.28 point less satisfied with life. This effect is reduced when controlling for other perceptions, although it may be underestimated because of the high nonresponse rate on this question (9.1 percent) compared to a nonresponse rate of only between 0.5 percent and 2 percent on other questions, partly reflecting fear of the government.

In summary, the same factors cited as reasons for the Arab Spring uprisings by the majority of respondents in Arab Barometer surveys (figure 5.9) also negatively and significantly affected the well-being of Arab people in the period immediately preceding the uprising (2009–10). These factors included dissatisfaction with standards of living, corruption in the form of nepotism or cronyism, and poor labor market conditions. These grievances are linked to Gurr's (1970) relative deprivation theory.[5] Better educated than their parents, young people expected to do better

FIGURE 5.9

Reasons for Arab Spring Based on Views in Developing MENA

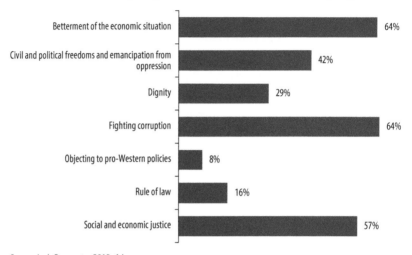

Source: Arab Barometer 2012–14.
Note: MENA = Middle East and North Africa.

than the previous generation but instead struggled to find good-quality jobs and were disappointed that no matter how hard they worked they could not get ahead (Arampatzi et al. 2015). Jobless young men could not hope to get married without a stable source of income (Bromley 2014). Huge progress in reducing and, in some cases, eliminating gender gaps in education, and steep declines in fertility rates, implied that Arab women were more prepared than ever before to participate in the labor market and contribute to economic life. The reality, however, was that unemployment rates among women were much higher than those among men (figure 5.4), and female labor force participation rates remained low (figure 5.5).

These results are echoed in statistics showing an increase in dissatisfaction with the quality of government services in developing Arab countries, and in the Arab Spring countries in particular (figure 5.10). The percentage of people dissatisfied with the availability of affordable housing rose most dramatically before the uprisings, but there was also an increase in the incidence of people dissatisfied with public transportation, the quality of health care, and the availability of quality jobs. In Arab Spring countries, the deterioration in average life satisfaction was also mostly driven by the increase in the percentage of people dissatisfied with their living conditions and the increased importance of perceptions about corruption for life satisfaction (Arampatzi et al. 2015).

FIGURE 5.10

Dissatisfaction with Government Services

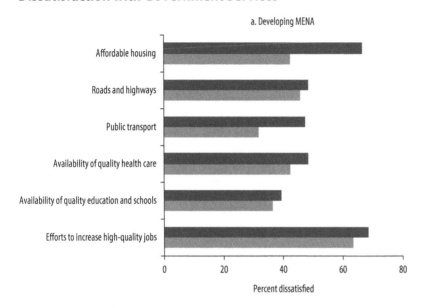

a. Developing MENA

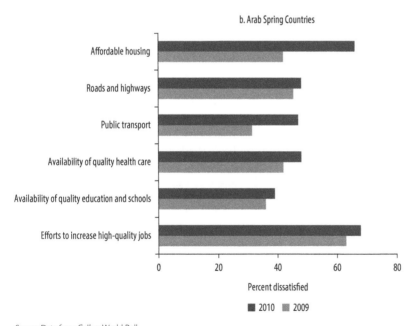

b. Arab Spring Countries

■ 2010 ■ 2009

Source: Data from Gallup World Poll.
Note: MENA = Middle East and North Africa.

Notes

1. One way to see this coercion is that violence was used to repress dissent during the time when the social contracts were supposedly working well, for example, in the Syrian Arab Republic (1980–82), the Republic of Yemen (1962–70), and the Arab Republic of Egypt (1977). Several studies document the use of repressive force in Syria (van Dam 2011), the Republic of Yemen (Dresh 2000), and throughout the region (Ayubi 1995).
2. The underemployed are respondents who are employed part time but who would like to work full time, whereas the unemployed respondents are not employed at all and are looking for job opportunities. Respondents who are out of the workforce include homemakers, students, and retirees.
3. The ruling elites controlled large parts of the private sector and profited from monopoly rights and cheap access to land and other resources (Cammett and Diwan 2013).
4. Arampatzi et al. (2015) also find that educational attainment and marriage with children are positively and significantly associated with life satisfaction in developing Arab countries. They also find that Arab women are, on average, happier than Arab men.
5. Gurr's (1970) idea of relative deprivation as a driver of civil unrest is linked to Galtung's (1966) notion of "status discrepancy" and Kriesberg's (1973) findings that most kinds of social behaviors, including manifestations of anger and dissent, are highly correlated with individuals' relative socioeconomic rank (Kriesberg 1973).

References

Angel-Urdinola, D. F., and A. Kuddo. 2011. "Key Characteristics of Employment Regulations in the Middle East and North Africa." MNA Knowledge and Learning Fast Brief 84, World Bank, Washington, DC.

Arampatzi, E., M. Burger, E. Ianchovichina, T. Röhricht, and R. Veenhoven. 2015. "Unhappy Development: Dissatisfaction with Life on the Eve of the Arab Spring." Policy Research Working Paper 7488, World Bank, Washington, DC.

Ayubi, N. 1995. *Over-stating the Arab State: Politics and Society in the Middle East.* New York: I. B. Tauris & Co. Ltd.

Behzadan, N., R. Chisik, H. Onder, and B. Battaile. 2017. "Does Inequality Drive the Dutch Disease? Theory and Evidence." *Journal of International Economics* 106: 103–18.

Bodor, A., D. Robalino, and M. Rutkowski. 2008. *How Mandatory Pensions Affect Labor Supply Decisions and Human Capital Accumulations: Options to Bridge the Gap between Economic Theory and Policy Analysis.* Washington, DC: World Bank.

Brixi, H., E. Lust, and M. Woolcock. 2015. *Trust, Voice, and Incentives: Learning from Local Success Stories in Service Delivery in the Middle East and North Africa.* Washington, DC: World Bank.

Bromley, R. 2014. "The 'Arab Spring' Stress Test: Diagnosing Reasons for the Revolt." Working Paper, University of Wisconsin-Madison.

Burger, M., E. Ianchovichina, and B. Rijkers. 2016. "Risky Business: Political Instability and Sectoral Greenfield Foreign Direct Investment in the Arab World." *World Bank Economic Review* 30 (2): 306–31.

Cammett, M. C., and I. Diwan. 2013. *The Political Economy of the Arab Uprisings*. New York: Perseus Books Group.

Campante, F. R., and D. Chor. 2012. "Why Was the Arab World Poised for Revolution? Schooling, Economic Opportunities, and the Arab Spring." *Journal of Economic Perspectives* 26: 167–88.

Chekir, H., and I. Diwan. 2012. "Distressed Whales on the Nile— Egypt Capitalists in the Wake of the 2010 Revolution." Working Paper 250, Center for International Development, Harvard University, Cambridge, MA.

Clark, A., A. Knabe, and S. Rätzel. 2010. "Boon or Bane? Others' Unemployment, Well-Being and Job Insecurity." *Labour Economics* 17: 52–61.

Clark, A. E., and A. J. Oswald. 1994. "Unhappiness and Unemployment." *Economic Journal* 104: 648–59.

Clements, B., D. Coady, S. Fabrizio, S. Gupta, T. Alleyne, and C. Sdralevich, eds. 2013. *Energy Subsidy Reform: Lessons and Implications*. Washington, DC: International Monetary Fund.

Devarajan, S., and L. Mottaghi. 2014. "Towards a New Social Contract." *MENA Economic Monitor*, World Bank, Washington, DC.

Di Tella, R., R. J. MacCulloch, and A. J. Oswald. 2003. "The Macroeconomics of Happiness." *Review of Economics and Statistics* 85: 809–27.

Dorn, D., J. Fischer, G. Kirchgässner, and A. Sousa-Poza. 2007. "Is It Culture or Democracy? The Impact of Democracy and Culture on Happiness." *Social Indicators Research* 82 (3): 505–26.

Dresh, P. 2000. *A History of Modern Yemen*. Cambridge, UK: Cambridge University Press.

Fereidouni, H. G., Y. Najdi, and R. Amiri. 2013. "Do Governance Factors Matter for Happiness in the MENA Region?" *International Journal of Social Economics* 12: 1028–40.

Freund, C., and M. Jaud. 2015. *Champions Wanted: Promoting Exports in the Middle East and North Africa*. World Bank: Washington, DC.

Frey, B. S., and A. Stutzer. 2000. "Happiness Prospers in Democracy." *Journal of Happiness Studies* 1: 79–102.

Gallie, D., and H. Russell. 1998. "Unemployment and Life Satisfaction: A Cross-Cultural Comparison." *European Journal of Sociology* 39: 248–80.

Galtung, J. 1966. "Rank and Social Integration: A Multidimensional Approach." In *Sociological Theories in Progress*, Vol. 1, edited by J. Berger, M. Zelditch, and B. Anderson. New York: Houghton Mifflin.

Gatti, R., D. Angel-Urdinola, J. Silva, and A. Bodor. 2013. *Striving for Better Jobs: The Challenge of Informality in the Middle East and North Africa*. Directions in Development. Washington, DC: World Bank.

Graham, C., and S. Pettinato. 2002. *Happiness and Hardship: Opportunity and Insecurity in New Market Economies*. Washington, DC: Brookings Institution Press.

Gurr, T. R. 1970. *Why Men Rebel*. Princeton, NJ: Princeton University Press.

Helliwell, J. F., R. Layard, and J. Sachs, eds. 2015. *World Happiness Report 2015*. New York: United Nations.

Hirschman, A. O. 1973. "The Changing Tolerance for Income Inequality in the Course of Economic Development, with a Mathematical Appendix by Michael Rothschild." *Quarterly Journal of Economics* 87 (4): 544–66.

Hoekman, B., and K. Sekkat. 2009. "Deeper Integration of Goods, Services, Capital and Labor Markets: A Policy Research Agenda for the MENA Region." ERF Policy Research Report 32, Economic Research Forum, Giza, Egypt.

Ianchovichina, E., L. Mottaghi, and S. Devarajan. 2015. *Inequality, Uprisings, and Conflict in the Arab World.* Washington, DC: World Bank.

IMF (International Monetary Fund). 2014. "Energy Subsidies in the Middle East and North Africa: Lessons for Reform." Middle East and Central Asia Department, International Monetary Fund, Washington, DC.

Inglehart, R., R. Foa, C. Peterson, and C. Welzel. 2008. "Development, Freedom, and Rising Happiness: A Global Perspective (1981–2007)." *Perspectives on Psychological Science* 3: 264–85.

Iqbal, F., and Y. Kiendrebeogo. Forthcoming. "The Determinants of Child Mortality Reduction in the Middle East and North Africa." *Middle East Development Journal.*

Kaufmann, D., A. Kraay, and M. Mastruzzi. 2011. "The Worldwide Governance Indicators: Methodology and Analytical Issues." *Hague Journal on the Rule of Law* 3 (02): 220–46.

Kriesberg, L. 1973. *The Sociology of Social Conflicts.* Upper Saddle River, NJ: Prentice Hall.

Lewbel, A. 2012. "Using Heteroscedasticity to Identify and Estimate Mismeasured and Endogenous Regressor Models." *Journal of Business and Economic Statistics* 30 (1): 67–80.

Malik, A., and B. Awadallah. 2013. "The Economics of the Arab Spring." *World Development* 45: 296–313.

OECD (Organisation for Economic Co-operation and Development). 2009. "Ownership Structures in MENA Countries: Listed Companies, State-Owned, Family Enterprises and Some Policy Implications." OECD, Paris. http://www.oecd.org/mena/investment/35402110.pdf.

Ott, J. C. 2010. "Good Governance and Happiness in Nations: Technical Quality Precedes Democracy and Quality Beats Size." *Journal of Happiness Studies* 11: 353–68.

Rijkers, B., H. Arouri, C. Freund, and A. Nucifora. 2014. "Which Firms Create the Most Jobs in Developing Countries? Evidence from Tunisia." *Labour Economics* 31 (C): 84–102.

Rijkers, B., C. Freund, and A. Nucifora. 2017. "All in the Family: State Capture in Tunisia." *Journal of Development Economics* 124 (C): 41–59.

Schiffbauer, M., A. Sy, S. Hussain, H. Sahnoun, and P. Keefer. 2015. *Jobs or Privileges: Unleashing the Employment Potential of the Middle East and North Africa.* MENA Development Report. Washington, DC: World Bank.

Van Dam, N. 2011. *The Struggle for Power in Syria: Politics and Society under Asad and the Ba'th Party.* New York : I. B. Tauris & Co. Ltd.

Veenhoven, R. 1989. *National Wealth and Individual Happiness.* Springer: Netherlands.

Verme, P. 2009. "Happiness, Freedom and Control." *Journal of Economic Behavior and Organization* 71: 146–61.

Verme, P., B. Milanovic, S. Al-Shawarby, S. El Tawila, M. Gadallah, and E. A. A. El-Majeed. 2014. *Inside Inequality in the Arab Republic of Egypt: Facts and Perceptions across People, Time, and Space*. Washington, DC: World Bank.

World Bank. 2013. *Fairness and Accountability: Engaging in Health Systems in the Middle East and North Africa*. Washington, DC: World Bank.

———. 2014. *The Unfinished Revolution: Tunisia Development Policy Review*. Washington, DC: World Bank.

PART 3

The Paradox of "Political Violence in Middle-Income Countries"

The Arab Spring initially brought hope for much-needed political, social, and economic change in the region. Just as the fall of the Berlin Wall ushered in a period of political and economic reform throughout Europe and Central Asia, the Arab Spring was expected to bring about democratic change and economic revival. However, soon after the initial protests toppled long-standing autocratic governments in the Arab Republic of Egypt, Libya, and the Republic of Yemen, it became clear that the Arab Spring transitions would be difficult and prolonged, and many would fail to change economies and societies for the better. Yet few people foresaw the gravity of the post–Arab Spring developments and the scale and intensity of devastation as bloody civil wars crippled several Arab states and violent extremist terrorist networks spread throughout the region.

This part of the study explores the reasons for these developments, looking in particular at the factors behind the paradox of "political violence in middle-income countries," defined as high-incidence of political violence in countries that do not match the profile of countries at risk for conflict. The literature on armed insurgencies argues that countries at risk for civil war tend to be poor (Fearon and Laitin 2003), politically unstable (Hegre et al. 2001), abundant in lootable resources and unskilled labor (Collier and Hoeffler 2002), and ethnically polarized (Montalvo and Reynal-Querol 2005; Esteban, Mayoral, and Ray 2012). With the exception of the Republic of Yemen, the Arab countries did not fit this profile. Most Arab countries were middle-income states and had made good development progress toward reducing extreme poverty (figure O.3), improving access to education and health, and keeping economic inequality at moderate levels (figure O.4). Except for Iraq and the Republic of Yemen, all other Arab countries ranked high in political stability according to *Foreign Policy*'s 2010 Failed States Index.[1]

TABLE P3.1

Average Indicators of External Intervention, Conflict, and Polarization

per country per 5-year period from 1960 to 2005

	External intervention	Conflict incidence	Religious polarization	Ethnic polarization
MENA	0.370	0.267	0.470	0.525
SSA	0.166	0.179	0.701	0.537
EAP	0.095	0.136	0.507	0.458
LAC	0.084	0.086	0.404	0.646

Sources: Abu Bader and Ianchovichina (2017) based on the following data sources: the global International Military Intervention data set for external intervention; the Peace Research Institute of Oslo data set for conflict incidence of moderate intensity; L'Etat des religions dans le monde and *The Statesman's Yearbook* for religious polarization; and the World Christian Encyclopedia for ethnic polarization.
Note: EAP = East Asia and Pacific; LAC = Latin America and the Caribbean; MENA = Middle East and North Africa; SSA = Sub-Saharan Africa.

Ranked 111th and 118th of 177 countries, respectively, Libya and Tunisia appeared to be among the stronger and less fragile countries in the world (Goodwin 2011).

Before the Arab Spring, the region remained resilient to economic and financial shocks. Most countries of the Middle East and North Africa (MENA) region weathered the global economic and financial crisis of 2008 better than countries in other parts of the world because the region was less integrated into the global economy through trade and finance (Ianchovichina et al. 2010). In addition, indicators of ethnic and religious polarization in the region suggested that, on average, the levels of polarization were moderate (table P3.1). In this context, the high incidence of civil conflict in the MENA region, both before and after the Arab Spring, presents a paradox.

This part of the study focuses on the aftermath of the Arab Spring. It examines the profile of protestors and the intensity and scale of the protests in chapter 6; the factors that in some cases escalated protests into armed insurgencies, as well as those that in other cases played a stabilizing role in chapter 7; and the development and economic consequences of these post–Arab Spring developments in chapter 8. The study concludes in chapter 8 with a discussion of the essential elements of a new social contract and a new model for security.

Note

1. The Failed States Index measures stability based on economic, political, and military indicators.

References

Abu Bader, S., and E. Ianchovichina. 2017. "Polarization, Foreign Military Interventions, and Civil Conflicts." Policy Research Working Paper 8248. World Bank, Washington, DC.

Collier, P., and A. Hoeffler. 2002. "On the Incidence of Civil War in Africa." *Journal of Conflict Resolution* 46 (1): 13–28.

Esteban, J., L. Mayoral, and D. Ray. 2012. "Ethnicity and Conflict: An Empirical Study." *American Economic Review* 102 (4): 1310–42.

Fearon, J., and D. Laitin. 2003. "Ethnicity, Insurgency, and Civil War." *American Political Science Review* 97 (1): 75–90.

Goodwin, J. 2011. "Why We Were Surprised (Again) by the Arab Spring." *Swiss Political Science Review* 17: 452–56.

Hegre, H., T. Ellingsen, S. Gates, and N. P. Gledisch. 2001 "Toward a Democratic Civil Peace? Democracy, Political Change, and Civil War, 1816–1992." *American Political Science Review* 95 (1): 33–48.

Ianchovichina, E., I. Mottaghi, K. Carey, N. Spivak, S. Farazi, and A. Silwal. 2010. "Middle East and North Africa Economic Update." World Bank Other Operational Studies 23977, World Bank, Washington, DC.

Montalvo, J., and M. Reynal-Querol. 2005. "Ethnic Polarization, Potential Conflict, and Civil Wars." *American Economic Review* 95 (3): 796–816.

CHAPTER 6

Arab Spring Protestors and Protests

Introduction

This chapter builds a profile of the Arab Spring demonstrators and discusses the incidence of protests and riots as a way of corroborating the findings in part 2 on broad-based grievances and the strong demand for change.

The Profile of Arab Spring Protestors

This section uses Arab Barometer data to construct a portrait of Arab Spring protesters. The collective data suggest that the typical Arab protestor was single, educated, relatively young (younger than 44), middle class, urban, and male (figure 6.1). Thus, mostly middle-class and relatively affluent people rose to protest the status quo. However, important differences across countries can be discerned. Compared with other age groups, protest participation rates were significantly higher among both youth and young middle-aged people (those between 30 and 44) in the Arab Republic of Egypt and the Republic of Yemen and mostly among youth in Tunisia and Libya (figure 6.1). The protest participation rate among students was significantly higher than that of other employment status groups (the employed, the unemployed, and those out of the workforce) only in Tunisia, reflecting the extremely high unemployment rates among educated youth. In all other countries, protest participation rates among the fully employed were higher than or as high as those of other employment status groups. These statistics indicate that protestors had a wider set of grievances, not just labor market concerns, and that support for the protests came from a diverse group of mostly young people who were middle class or affluent. In Libya and Tunisia, protest participation

FIGURE 6.1

The Profile of the Arab Spring Protestors

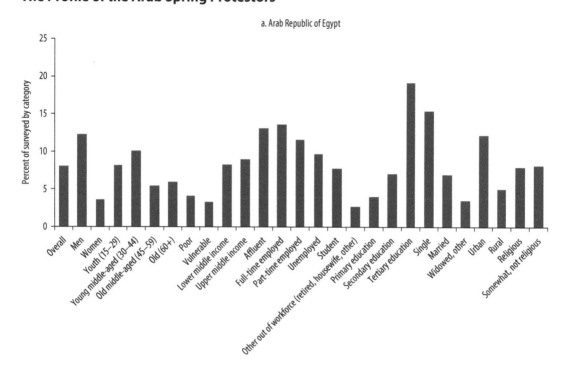

a. Arab Republic of Egypt

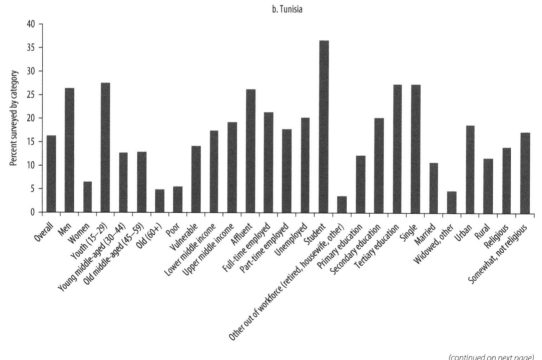

b. Tunisia

(continued on next page)

FIGURE 6.1

The Profile of the Arab Spring Protestors   *Continued*

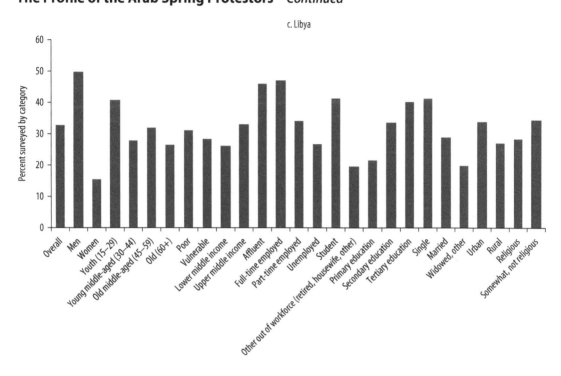

c. Libya

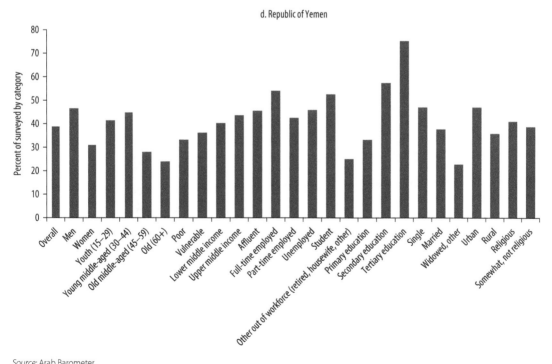

d. Republic of Yemen

Source: Arab Barometer.

rates were lower among religious people than among less religious residents; such differences were not evident in Egypt and the Republic of Yemen (figure 6.1).

Arab Spring Protests and Riots

In 2011, the number of protests and riots escalated dramatically (from a low base) throughout the region, but the incidence and intensity of these events and participation in them varied widely across Arab countries (figure 6.2). Protests and riots occurred most often in Egypt, the Syrian Arab Republic, and the Republic of Yemen; in these three countries about 240 protests and riots took place during 2011 (figure 6.2). Riots were common in Egypt, Tunisia, and the Republic of Yemen, but in general the number of protests was much larger than the number of riots. The per capita number of large protests and riots was highest in Libya, Syria, and the Republic of Yemen (figure 6.2), where the Arab Spring protests subsequently turned into large-scale civil wars.

Protest participation rates were highest in Libya and the Republic of Yemen, where approximately a third of the population took part in Arab Spring demonstrations, and lowest in Algeria, Jordan, and Lebanon (figure 6.3). Within Northern Africa, where data on fatalities during

FIGURE 6.2

Incidence of Protests and Riots in Developing MENA

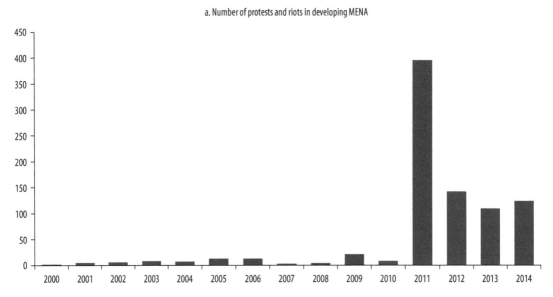

a. Number of protests and riots in developing MENA

(continued on next page)

FIGURE 6.2

Incidence of Protests and Riots in Developing MENA *Continued*

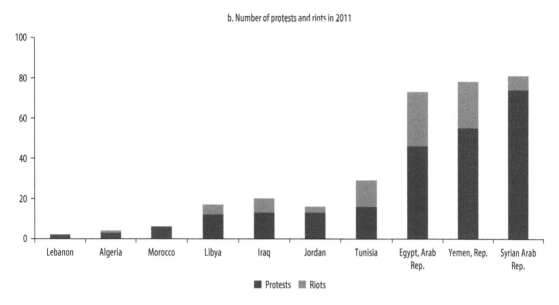

b. Number of protests and riots in 2011

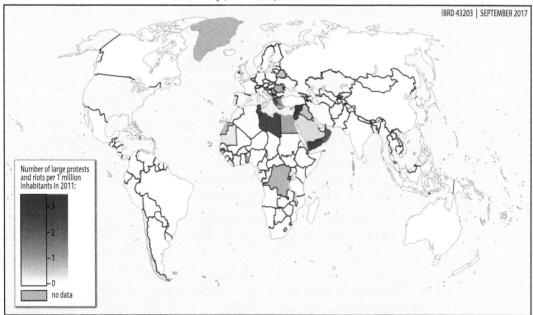

c. Number of large protests and riots per 1 million inhabitants in 2011

Source: Data on number of protests and riots from Databanks International's Cross-National Time-Series Data Archive.
Note: MENA = Middle East and North Africa.

FIGURE 6.3

Participation in Protests and Riots in Developing MENA, 2011–12

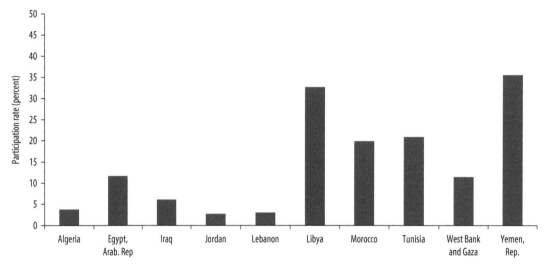

Source: Data on protest participation rates come from Arab Barometer, Wave III, except in Egypt and Tunisia where data are from Wave II.
Note: Databanks International's Cross-National Time-Series Data Archive records protests and riots with 100 or more participants.

protests are available, the intensity of protests, measured by the average number of casualties per protest, was highest in Egypt and lowest in Morocco (figure 6.4). In Egypt, close to 20 people, on average, died in each protest in 2011. The high number of fatalities in Egypt is striking, given that only a small share of the population participated in demonstrations during the 2011–12 period, but it is consistent with the large share of riots (close to 40 percent) (figure 6.2) in the total number of demonstrations because riots tend to be violent and protests tend to be peaceful.

Although a small share of people took part in the protests, support for them was much broader, especially in the Arab Spring countries, where the vast majority of people supported the protestors' calls for government change (figure 6.5). In Egypt and Libya, more than 80 percent of those surveyed supported the protestors, while in Tunisia and the Republic of Yemen popular support exceeded 70 percent and 60 percent, respectively. Support for political change was weakest in Jordan and Morocco, as well as in Algeria, Iraq, and Lebanon.

People did not participate in the protests for a variety of reasons (figure 6.6). In Algeria, Jordan, Lebanon, and Morocco, most people did not attend the protests because they did not care about them. In most countries, with the exception of Jordan and Lebanon, between 5 percent and 10 percent of the people did not participate in the protests because

FIGURE 6.4

Intensity of Protests and Riots in Developing MENA, 2011

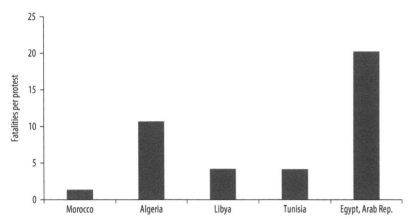

Source: Data on fatalities are obtained from Armed Conflict Location & Event Data Project (http://www
.acleddata.com/) and are available only for countries in North Africa.
Note: MENA = Middle East and North Africa.

FIGURE 6.5

Population Supporting Protestors' Calls for Political Change

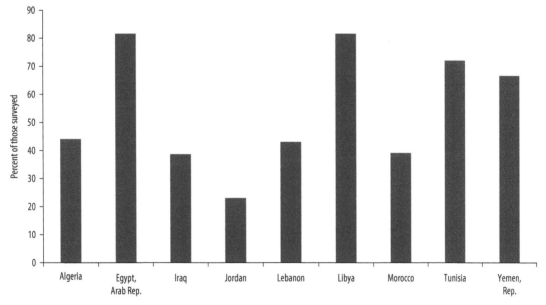

Source: Gallup World Poll 2012.

they were afraid. Divisions in society were starkest in the Republic of
Yemen, where 25 percent of nonparticipants did not agree with the demonstrations and another 15 percent did not know whom to support. In
Libya, nearly half of the nonparticipants did not identify a reason for not
participating in the protests.

FIGURE 6.6

Reasons for Not Participating in the Arab Spring Protests, by Economy

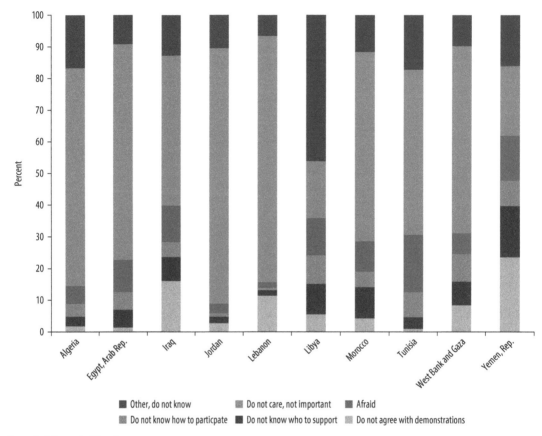

Source: Arab Barometer, Wave III.

In Egypt and Tunisia, the share of those who did not participate in the protests because they did not care about them was smaller among the more affluent in society than among the poorer bottom 40 percent of the population (figure 6.7). This finding of stronger demand for change among the middle class than among the poorest segments of the population in the two countries where the Arab Spring arrived first is in line with the arguments in part 2 of this study that a broken social contract rather than high inequality led to the Arab Spring. In Libya, no substantial differences in the answers for nonparticipation across income classes were evident, so support for change was broad-based. The affluent and the upper-middle classes were more likely not to agree with the protestors than the poor and vulnerable (the bottom 40 percent) only in the Republic of Yemen, but the poor and vulnerable were more likely not to know whom to support (figure 6.6).

These statistics suggest that demand for change was strongest in the Arab Spring countries (Egypt, Syria, Libya, Tunisia, and the Republic of Yemen),

FIGURE 6.7

Reasons for Not Participating in the Arab Spring Protests, by Welfare Group and Country

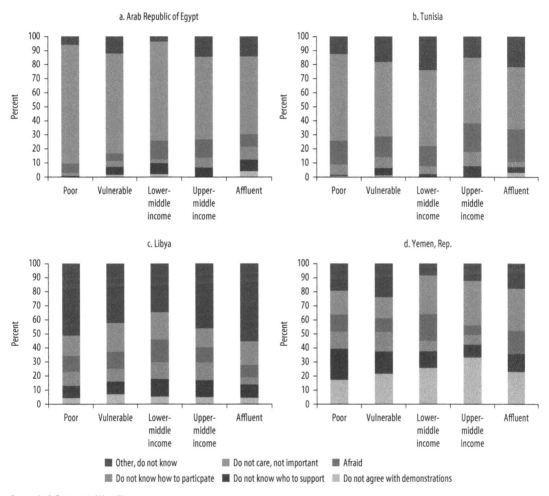

Source: Arab Barometer, Wave III.
Note: The welfare groups are defined by splitting the survey population into quintiles. This definition of the welfare groups differs from the one presented in parts 1 and 2.

where grievances associated with the broken social contract were most pronounced and broadly shared and where per capita incidence of protests and riots, participation in these events, and popular support for them were highest in the MENA region. Chapter 7 explores whether divisions along ethnic, religious, and regional lines contributed to the transformation of demonstrations and riots into full-fledged civil wars. Chapter 7 also examines divisions in society and the supply-side factors for change that affected conflict outcomes, including the strength of governance institutions that matter for conflict and external interventions by global and regional players.

The Aftermath of the Arab Spring

Introduction

In 2011, the Arab people spoke loudly and clearly, voicing grievances crucial to their well-being and calling for change. Yet, the Arab uprisings did not deliver the change people hoped for; instead, the situation deteriorated significantly throughout the Middle East and North Africa (MENA). In Libya, the Syrian Arab Republic, and the Republic of Yemen the uprisings mutated into civil wars; in Iraq, the civil war recurred and violent extremist networks spread throughout the country and neighboring areas; in the rest of the Arab countries, many of the factors that made people unhappy before the Arab Spring uprisings remained, and the economic situation worsened considerably. This chapter discusses the factors that helped some countries remain stable and those factors that transformed the protests into armed insurgencies.

During the aftermath of the Arab Spring, most governments relied on a combination of redistributive policies and different forms of coercion to address the demand for change. Where demand for change was least intense, rule-of-law institutions were strong, and generous redistributive schemes were implemented,[1] governments were able to patch up the cracks in the social contract and prevent the escalation of protests into uprisings. By contrast, in countries where the contract was broken and demand for change was most intense, protests quickly grew into uprisings. In the countries with the weakest law-and-order institutions, uprisings grew into armed insurgencies (for example, in Libya, Syria, and the Republic of Yemen) or civil conflict recurred despite efforts to strengthen stability (for example, Iraq). This argument is consistent with the writings of Murshed (2009), who argues that civil war is a reflection of the breakdown or degeneration of a social contract governing interaction between various groups within a country. Finally, in some countries, uncoordinated external military interventions created conditions that led to escalation of armed insurgencies into intense civil wars.

State Responses to the Arab Spring

Most Arab governments responded to the eruption of popular anger using redistributive policies to quell social unrest and thus patch the cracks in the social contract. Documented extensively in World Bank (2011), the fiscal measures used by governments to appease the public included a mix of wage, pension, and subsidy increases; transfers in the form of grants; the creation of thousands of jobs in the public sector; and, in some cases, the announcement of new infrastructure programs. The fiscal cost of these measures was highest in Algeria and the oil-rich Gulf Cooperation Council (GCC) countries, especially Saudi Arabia, where it reached close to 20 percent of gross domestic product (GDP). In other Arab countries, the cost was more modest, varying between 1 percent and 5 percent of GDP (World Bank 2011).

Post–Arab Spring intraregional GCC assistance supported the redistributive policies in poorer countries in the region. The assistance came in the form of a variety of instruments: grants, hard-currency deposits, fuel products, loans, and investments. The support was extended in a speedy manner and was mostly granted bilaterally rather than multilaterally through Gulf institutions. Ample petrodollar savings, built up following years of high oil prices, enabled the provision of generous support to some of the politically and strategically important countries, including Jordan, Morocco, and Oman, while support for Tunisia was modest. Gulf assistance to the Arab Republic of Egypt came from different sources during and after the Morsi government. Qatar supported the government of the Muslim Brotherhood, whereas Saudi Arabia, the United Arab Emirates, Kuwait, and Oman viewed the rise of the Muslim Brotherhood as a threat and pledged generous support for the regime of General al-Sisi (Khalifa Isaac 2015; Lynch 2016). According to official Egyptian sources, between July 2013 and March 2015, Egypt received about $35 billion in assistance funds from these four GCC states, in addition to numerous investment contracts (Khalifa Isaac 2015).

The weak demand for change and the generous redistribution worked to prevent escalation of protests into uprisings in the GCC countries, the other two monarchies, Jordan and Morocco, and Algeria. In addition, the royal Arab states relied on relatively strong rule-of-law institutions to preserve stability (figure 7.1). Monarchs, seen as legitimate heads of state, were outside the field of contestation, and protestors in the

FIGURE 7.1

Quality of Governance Institutions in Arab Economies, 2010

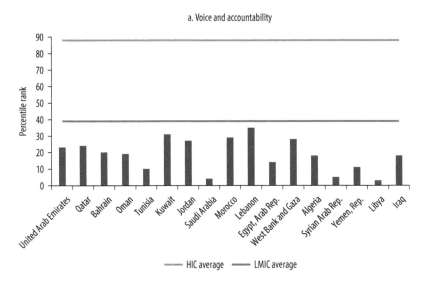

a. Voice and accountability

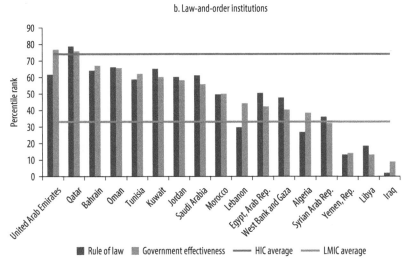

b. Law-and-order institutions

Source: World Bank, Worldwide Governance Indicators database.
Note: HIC = high-income countries; LMIC = lower-middle-income countries.

Arab monarchies were calling mostly for internal reforms (Williamson and Abadeer 2014).[2] However, any attempts to appease popular anger, including through redistribution, failed in the other Arab countries. There, demonstrations resulted in uprisings, which in nearly all cases except Syria managed to topple long-standing dictators.

The World Bank's Worldwide Governance Indicators are useful in providing empirical evidence on the nature and limitations of the Arab security approach. As discussed in chapter 4 of the World Bank's World Development Report (World Bank 2017), countries use four types of governance institutions for security: (1) sanction-and-deterrence institutions, which deter and reduce incentives for violent behavior; (2) redistributive institutions, which redistribute resources; (3) power-sharing institutions for inclusive constitution-making process and political representation; and (4) dispute-settlement institutions, which, when they are fair, reduce incentives to use violence. However, Arab countries had mainly developed just the first two types of institutions, which were also essential for the old social contract. In their two-pronged governance model for security, institutions for inclusion and voice remained underdeveloped. The Worldwide Governance Indicator's voice and accountability index can be used as a proxy for the extent of power sharing or inclusion because it captures perceptions of the extent to which citizens are able to participate in selecting their government, as well as of freedom of expression, freedom of association, and a free media. This index was uniformly low and substantially below the level expected even in lower-middle-income countries (figure 7.1, panel a). Within the region, power sharing was limited to the greatest extent in Libya, followed by Saudi Arabia, Syria, the Republic of Yemen, and Egypt; and it was least restricted in Lebanon, followed by Kuwait, Morocco, and Jordan.

As demand for change increased, the quality of law-and-order institutions became increasingly important to the ability of the old regimes to stay in power and retain their monopoly on violence. The Rule-of-Law and Government Effectiveness components of the World Governance Indicators serve as proxies for the strength of law-and-order institutions because they capture, among other things, perceptions of the extent to which citizens have confidence in the authorities' ability to protect them and reduce the likelihood of violence (Kaufmann, Kraay, and Mastruzzi 2010). Lack of confidence in the ability or willingness of the police and military to protect the people can give rise to incentives of various nongovernment groups to challenge the regime. On the eve of the Arab Spring, the Worldwide Governance Indicators for rule of law and government effectiveness indicated that the quality of law-and-order institutions was worst in Iraq, where armed conflict had persisted for years, and in the Republic of Yemen, followed by Libya and Syria (figure 7.1, panel b). The distance of the rankings of Iraq, Libya, and the Republic of Yemen from those expected for their level of development is stark and suggests that the risk of political violence during the Arab Spring period in these three countries was high.

However, the rankings of Arab countries on this aspect of institutional quality exhibited great heterogeneity (figure 7.1, panel b). In Syria, the quality of law-and-order institutions was only slightly lower than that expected for its level of development, but other factors tipped the balance in favor of political violence. One of these factors was the government's use of extreme violence to repress the protestors.[3] This was expected in Syria, as well as in Libya, where repression and lack of voice and accountability were extreme (figure 7.1, top panel) and the regime fostered military loyalty through ethnic or sectarian preferences (see McLauchlin 2010). These preferences enabled the regime to retain a core of loyal military supporters who were willing to violently repress protests because their fates were tied to the fate of the regime. In addition, the Syrian regime could not use redistribution to appease the population because its oil wealth was becoming depleted[4] and the Gulf states did not offer financial assistance to the regime. At the same time, social protection needs had grown dramatically because large swaths of rural areas were suffering the effects of the worst drought in Syria's history (Femia and Werrell 2012), forcing thousands of rural inhabitants to migrate internally to the outskirts of Damascus and other large cities in the country. In Egypt and Tunisia, the quality of law-and-order institutions was considerably better than that of those in Iraq, Libya, Syria, and the Republic of Yemen. Tunisia's institutions, in particular, were comparable to those in the high-income GCC countries. Furthermore, in both of these countries, the populations were homogeneous and included mostly Sunni Muslims. Therefore, the militaries in these two countries were connected to the regimes only by individual incentives, not by ethnic or sectarian ties. Because the initial mass protests signaled regime weakness, the military and police were encouraged to abandon the regimes rather than repress the protestors during the initial demonstrations.[5]

This analysis suggests that, in the immediate aftermath of the Arab Spring, the risk of political violence was highest in Libya, Syria, and the Republic of Yemen—the Arab countries where demand for change was strong, repression was widespread, inclusion was limited, and rule-of-law institutions were weakest. Thus, only in the Arab Spring countries with the weakest state governance institutions for security did protests and riots escalate into armed uprisings.

Foreign Interventions, Identity-Based Polarization, and High-Intensity Civil Wars

MENA has been a conflict-prone region for decades. Even before the Arab Spring, the probability of political violence was much higher in parts of MENA (for example, Algeria, Lebanon, the West Bank and Gaza) than in the rest of the world (table P3.1). After the Arab Spring, as argued in the previous section, the risk of political violence rose substantially, reflecting both a broken social contract and a broken governance model for security. During the same time, the incidence of Arabs who morally justified the use of extreme violence against civilians also rose substantially, although such views were also found elsewhere in the world (figure 7.2). Using Gallup World Poll data from several, mostly developing, Arab countries,[6] Kiendrebeogo and Ianchovichina (2016) find that Arabs willing to sacrifice their own lives for their beliefs were significantly more likely to express radical ideas and support violence against civilians.

The economic literature emphasizes different explanatory factors for civil war, but virtually all relate to domestic factors and processes. Theoretical studies of internal conflict focus on grievance-motivated rebellions (Gurr 1970), the factors creating opportunities for collective action in mobilization (Tilly 1978), the role of rents from conflict in promoting support for violence (Collier and Hoeffler 2004), dormant traumas that can be awakened and used as a tool to motivate identity-based hatred and conflict (Diab 2015), and horizontal distributional factors such as ethnic polarization (Esteban and Ray 2011; Esteban, Mayoral and Ray 2012).

FIGURE 7.2

Incidence of Individuals Who Morally Justify Attacks Targeting Civilians, by Region

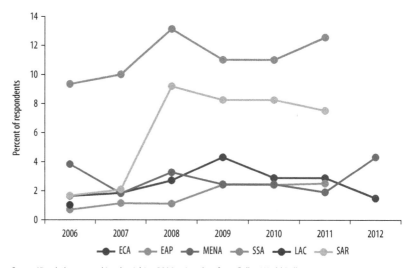

Source: Kiendrebeogo and Ianchovichina 2016, using data from Gallup World Poll.
Note: EAP = East Asia and Pacific; ECA = Europe and Central Asia; LAC = Latin America and the Caribbean; MENA = Middle East and North Africa; SAR = South Asia; SSA = Sub-Saharan Africa.

This literature largely overlooks the role of transnational factors on conflict incidence (Regan 2010), despite the importance given to international factors in popular accounts of civil wars (McNulty 1999). Existing studies focus on the effect of external interventions on the duration of civil wars (Elbadawi and Sambanis 2000) and civil war settlement (Walter 1997; Gleditsch and Beardsley 2004). Elbadawi and Sambanis (2000) provide strong evidence that external interventions tend to lengthen civil conflict, irrespective of whether the intervention is in the form of direct military involvement, aid, or sanctions, or whether it is designed to be neutral or to favor the government or the opposition (Regan 2000). Several explanations for this effect have been put forward, with the most popular explanation linked to expected utility (Lake and Rothchild 1998). Foreign intervention provides the resources necessary for one or both sides to carry out insurgency, which lowers the opportunity cost of participating in the war, potentially making rival groups optimistic about the likelihood of a military victory and creating commitment problems.[7]

Few studies explore the question of how external interventions influence the incidence of civil wars. Cetinyan (2002) finds that external support does not affect war incidence, but it influences the terms of settlement in the event conflict occurs. Gershenson (2002) also looks at this issue but with regard to sanctions, not direct military intervention. He finds that strong sanctions can compel the state to consider rebel demands whereas weak sanctions against the state can weaken the rebels' position. Gleditsch (2007) examines how transnational contagion from neighboring states affects the risk of conflict in a country and concludes that regional factors strongly influence the risk of civil conflict.

Abu Bader and Ianchovichina (2017) look at how nonneutral and nonhumanitarian external military interventions alter the balance of power among potential warring groups by altering the resources available to them and their probability of winning. They find extremely high incidence of such external interventions per MENA country relative to countries in other developing regions during the past five decades (table P3.1) and show that religious polarization in the presence of such interventions increases the risk of large-scale civil wars (figure 7.3). There is no evidence of such an effect for neutral and humanitarian military interventions. Stated differently, only nonneutral and nonhumanitarian military external interventions in the MENA region tend to activate religious-based hatred, amplify polarization along sectarian lines, and create incentives to raise resources for civil wars.

The events of the post–Arab Spring period are consistent with the findings in Abu Bader and Ianchovichina (2017). External interventions of

FIGURE 7.3

Marginal Effect of External Intervention on Probability of Conflict

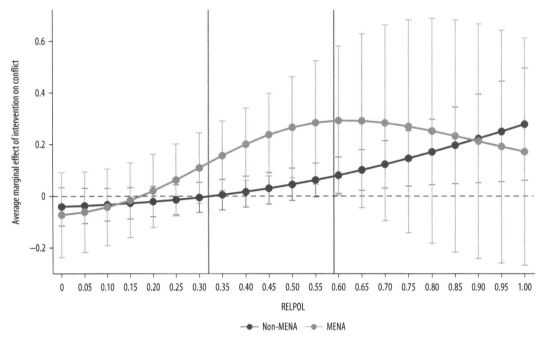

Source: Abu Bader and Ianchovichina 2017.
Note: The vertical lines mark the range of religious polarization values for which the marginal effect of intervention on conflict is statistically different from zero. Religious polarization is an index between 0 and 1, with values closer to 1 indicating a higher degree of polarization. MENA = Middle East and North Africa.

various types (military, economic, and political) peaked in the aftermath of the Arab Spring as regional powers saw an opportunity to increase their influence in the region (Lynch 2016). These interventions occurred in an uncoordinated and competitive fashion, increasing the risk of polarization along sectarian lines and creating conditions for large-scale civil wars, even though the Arab Spring protests were initially domestically grown and represented broad-based dissatisfaction with the status quo. Most interventions have not been neutral, and their objectives have changed as the situations on the ground have evolved from aiming to change regimes (as in Libya, Syria, and the Republic of Yemen) to supporting regimes (Iraq and the Republic of Yemen) (Lynch 2016). They were extended by a multitude of stakeholders from multiple countries and included a mix of support to rebel groups, direct military operations, economic sanctions, and media and diplomacy campaigns. In Syria, external interventions created a competitive proxy war in which each intervention on one side triggered a response from the backers of the other side (see Lynch 2016).

Overlapping Horizontal Divisions

Sectarian divisions or cleavages in society can create conditions for civil war and offer an opportunity to external groups to intervene and destabilize countries, further increasing polarization among different stakeholders. Work on regional and ethnic inequality (Alesina et al. 2016) and ethnic polarization (Montalvo and Reynal-Querol 2005; Esteban, Mayoral, and Ray 2012) provides valuable insights. The persistence of a regional divide could lead to conflict, as argued by Lipton (1977), especially in low-income countries; and regional divides have been on the rise according to Kanbur and Venables (2005). The case study literature offers many examples of an association between conflict and "horizontal inequality," or inequality that coincides with sectarian cleavages. Deprivation along ethnic, religious, and sectarian lines may enhance group grievances and thus facilitate mobilization for conflict (Stewart 2000, 2002).

One of the few cross-country studies, by Ostby (2008), finds support for Stewart's case studies by systematically testing ethnically based horizontal inequalities across several developing countries. In a subsequent study, Ostby, Nordas, and Rod (2009) apply geographic information system techniques to Demographic and Health Surveys to construct new disaggregated data on welfare and socioeconomic inequalities between and within subnational regions in 22 Sub-Saharan African countries and combine these data with geographical data on the location of conflict zones for the period 1986–2004. They find that the onset of conflict is more likely in regions with (1) low levels of education, (2) strong relative deprivation regarding household assets, (3) strong intraregional inequalities, and (4) combined presence of natural resources and relative deprivation.

However, the link between ethnic and religious diversity and social conflict has been hotly contested. Fearon and Laitin (2003) do not find a link between ethnic heterogeneity and conflict, but others insist that ethnic cleavages may increase the risk of conflict (Ellingsen 2000; Cederman and Girardin 2007; Montalvo and Reynal-Querol 2005) and the duration of civil wars (Collier, Hoeffler, and Soderbom 2004).[8] Arguing that there is less violence in highly homogeneous and highly heterogeneous societies, and more conflict in societies where a large ethnic minority lives side by side with an ethnic majority, Montalvo and Reynal-Querol (2005) show that ethnic polarization,[9] not ethnic fractionalization,[10] is a significant explanatory variable for the incidence of civil war. They conclude that ethnic polarization has robust and significant explanatory power for civil wars in the presence of other indexes of fractionalization and polarization, while the statistical significance of religious polarization depends on the particular specification and, as shown in Abu Bader and Ianchovichina (2017), on the presence of non-neutral and nonhumanitarian foreign interventions, which tend to amplify religious polarization, increasing the risk of high-intensity civil wars. Esteban and Ray (2011) theoretically formalize the link between distributional measures and conflict incidence and test these links empirically in Esteban, Mayoral, and Ray (2012). Assuming no external intervention, they find that all three indexes of ethnic distribution—polarization, fractionalization, and the Gini-Greenberg index—are significant correlates of conflict.[11]

Horizontal inequality—inequality along regional and ethnic lines—was substantial in many Arab countries, despite low-to-moderate expenditure inequality before 2011. Regional and rural-urban disparities were substantial contributors to overall inequality during the previous two decades (figure 7.4). Regional differences were most significant in Egypt and Iraq (accounting for 20 percent or more of expenditure inequality), and rural-urban inequality contributed the most to expenditure inequality in Egypt and Tunisia. The contribution of spatial differences declined over time in Egypt, but increased in most developing MENA economies, including Jordan, Syria, Tunisia, and the Republic of Yemen (figure 7.4).

FIGURE 7.4

Decomposition of Expenditure Inequality, by Household Attributes

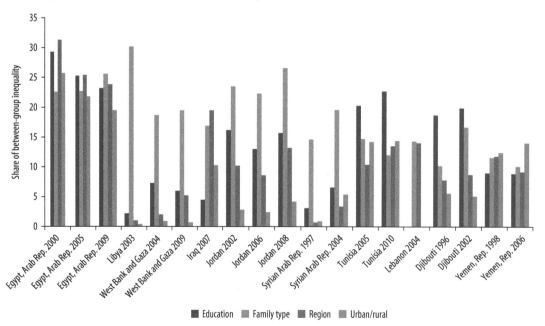

Source: Hassine 2014.

In Syria, despite the overall increase in average incomes in the 1990s and the first decade of the 2000s, household expenditures in northern Syria lagged behind, reflecting to a large extent the devastating effect of the worst drought in the country's history. Similarly, people located in the center west of Tunisia, where the Arab Spring revolts began, saw little improvement of average incomes over time.

Alesina, Michalopoulos, and Papaioannou (2016) investigate the link between spatial and ethnic inequality. In their view, high ethnic inequality poses a particularly serious problem because it hampers development by generating sectarian hatred and envy, barriers to social mobility, a sense of unfairness, and, in many cases, conflict. They explore the origins and consequences of between-ethnic-group inequality across countries by combining satellite images of nighttime luminosity with the historical homelands of ethnolinguistic groups. According to them, it is ethnic inequality, not spatial inequality per se or ethnic fractionalization, that has a significant and negative association with socioeconomic development, although, naturally, ethnic inequality (of the type they measure in their paper)[12] is positively correlated with spatial inequality (figure 7.5).

FIGURE 7.5

Ethnic Inequality and Spatial Inequality

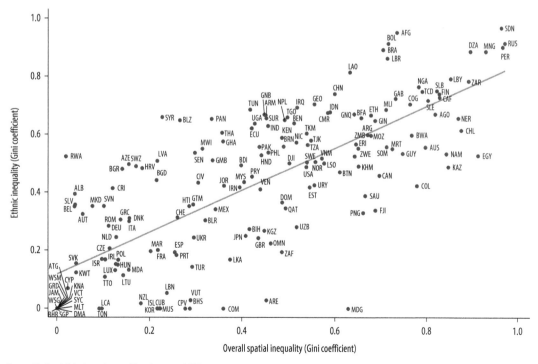

Source: Alesina, Michalopoulos, and Papaioannou 2016.

Using the data in Alesina, Michalopoulos, and Papaioannou (2016), it can be seen that in Iraq and in nearly all Arab Spring countries inequality among ethnic groups in regions outside urban areas has been higher than ethnic inequality in countries with similar levels of spatial inequality. In Syria and Tunisia, ethnic inequality was also much higher than spatial inequality (figure 7.5). By contrast, Egypt, Lebanon, Morocco, and the GCC countries (for example, Saudi Arabia, Oman, and the United Arab Emirates) have low ethnic inequality relative to that of other countries with similar levels of spatial inequality and relative to their own spatial inequality. In Jordan, ethnic inequality has been moderate and in line with the extent of spatial inequality. Worldwide, conflict-torn Sudan and Afghanistan stand out as having the highest degree of ethnic and regional inequality.

It is important to note that the data on ethnic inequality in Alesina, Michalopoulos, and Papaioannou (2016) exclude information from urban areas. Therefore, these data are less relevant to understanding the roots of the Arab Spring. In most MENA countries the majority of the population is urban and the demonstrations and riots, which started in urban centers, represented the grievances of mostly urban dwellers (figure 6.1). Moreover, overall intragroup distributional measures from other sources suggest, on average, that polarization along ethnic and religious lines in MENA has been moderate and lower than in other regions (table P3.1). However, the data used by Alesina, Michalopoulos, and Papaioannou (2016) provide valuable insights about the channels through which external interventions succeeded in gaining support among different ethnic or sectarian groups in parts of Iraq, Libya, Syria, and the Republic of Yemen. External military interventions appear to have enflamed hatred and polarization along ethnic and sectarian lines by taking advantage of the lagging status of regions far away from large urban areas, particularly those in proximity to fragile states (such as Iraq).

What Explains the Arab Paradox of "Political Violence in Middle-Income Countries"?

The discussion in this chapter points to two reasons behind the Arab middle-income conflict paradox, defined as high incidence of civil conflict in middle-income countries that have been stable for years and do not match the profile of countries at risk for civil conflict (table P3.1). The first reason is linked to domestic factors, including the breakdown in the social contract and the weakness in the governance institutions for security. Most cross-country economic studies on conflict assume that economic development and the development of strong governance institutions happen in parallel. However, the link between economic development and institutional quality is weaker in resource-rich countries than elsewhere in the world, as suggested by the flatter trend line for commodity exporters in figure 7.6. The "resource curse" literature provides an explanation for this weaker link. Natural wealth often strengthens authoritarian regimes and enables them to rely on resource rents rather than on taxation for redistribution. With low taxes, citizens have fewer incentives to demand accountability and better-quality institutions. In addition, the ruling elites have incentives to weaken civil society and the private sector and no incentives to improve the quality and inclusiveness of governance institutions. They benefit from resource rents and use them to buy political support through redistributive policies and to finance the rule-of-law authorities to keep citizens in check. In short, in resource-rich Arab states, as in many other resource-rich countries around the world, the average level of income per capita is a poor proxy for the quality of governance institutions and a poor

FIGURE 7.6

Economic Development and Institutional Quality

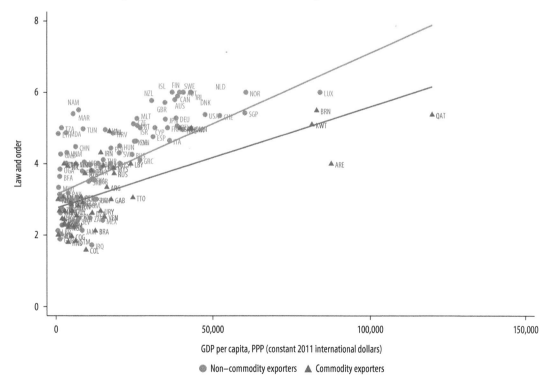

Sources: World Bank, World Development Indicators for GDP per capita; International Country Risk Guide for law and order.
Note: GDP = gross domestic product; PPP = purchasing power parity.

predictor of conflict. As shown in figure 7.1, governance institutions in Arab countries are much weaker than those in other countries with similar average per capita incomes.

The second reason for the paradox has to do with foreign factors, namely the high incidence of nonhumanitarian and nonneutral external interventions after the Arab Spring. These interventions exacerbated horizontal polarization along ethnic and religious lines and increased the risk of high-intensity civil conflicts. The motives behind these interventions are beyond the scope of this study.

Notes

1. In the Gulf Cooperation Council (GCC) countries, redistributive policies were possible because of ample fiscal space. In other Arab states, such as Jordan and Morocco, foreign transfers from the GCC states enabled governments to use redistributive policies during the transition period.
2. Of the region's eight monarchies, only Bahrain experienced a substantial uprising. Of the region's eight oil-wealthy regimes, two experienced uprisings—Bahrain and Libya. Of the six countries in the region that were oil poor and did not have hereditary monarchies, four experienced uprisings—Egypt, Syria, Tunisia, and the Republic of Yemen.
3. Lynch (2016) notes that in the first days of protests the Syrian government adopted a mixed strategy of token political reform and selectively inflicted violence and passed reforms that resembled those in Jordan and Morocco. He revised the constitution, released political prisoners, and ended the 50-year-old state of emergency. These reform efforts, however, lacked credibility.
4. In the 2000s Syria lost its status as a net oil exporter.
5. In both Egypt and Tunisia, the state was able to retain its monopoly on violence, but only in Tunisia did the transition lead to a working power-sharing arrangement, which can be attributed to Tunisia's more advanced power-sharing governance institutions and the balance of power between secular and Islamist parties.
6. These countries are Algeria, Egypt, Iraq, Lebanon, Qatar, Tunisia, and the Republic of Yemen.
7. Fearon (2004) makes similar arguments while Cunningham (2006) argues that uncoordinated multiple external interventions may impede a negotiated settlement, thereby prolonging civil conflict.
8. Collier, Hoeffler, and Soderbom (2004) argue that the duration of civil wars is positively, though nonmonotonically, related to the level of ethnic fractionalization of the warring society. The implication is that polarized societies would generate longer civil wars because the cost of coordinating a rebellion for a long enough period could be prohibitively high in very diverse societies.
9. Polarization measures capture the distance of the group distribution from the bipolar one in which the population is split in half into two large groups.
10. Fractionalization measures capture the extent of diversity in a country or society.

11. This result holds under the assumption that the resources committed by the warring groups come only from individual efforts within countries and that each warring group's probability of winning equals its population share (Esteban and Ray 2011).

12. Their data focus on ancestral lands and exclude large urban centers because these areas are ethnically diverse.

References

Abu Bader, S., and E. Ianchovichina. 2017. "Polarization, Foreign Military Interventions, and Civil Conflicts." Policy Research Working Paper 8248, World Bank, Washington, DC.

Albornoz, F., and E. Hauk. 2014. "Civil War and U.S. Foreign Influence." *Journal of Development Economics* 110: 64–78.

Alesina, A., S. Michalopoulos, and E. Papaioannou. 2016. "Ethnic Inequality." *Journal of Political Economy* 124 (2): 428–88.

Cederman, L., and L. Girardin. 2007. "Beyond Fractionalization: Mapping Ethnicity onto National Insurgencies." *American Political Science Review* 101 (1): 173–85.

Cetinyan, R. 2002. "Ethnic Bargaining in the Shadow of Third Party Intervention." *International Organization* 56 (3): 645–77.

Collier, P., and A. Hoeffler. 2004. "Greed and Grievance in Civil War." *Oxford Economic Papers* 56 (4): 563–95.

Collier, P., A. Hoeffler, and M. Soderbom. 2004. "On the Duration of Civil War." *Journal of Peace Research* 41 (3): 253–73.

Cunningham, D. 2006. "Veto Players and Civil War Duration." *American Journal of Political Science* 50 (4): 875–92.

Diab, K. 2015. "The Ghost of Conflicts Past, Present and Future." Al Jazeera Opinion Piece, August 27.

Elbadawi, I., and N. Sambanis. 2000. "External Interventions and the Duration of Civil Wars." Policy Research Working Paper 2433, World Bank, Washington, DC.

Ellingsen, T. 2000. "Colorful Community or Ethnic Witches' Brew? Multiethnicity and Domestic Conflict During and After the Cold War." *Journal of Conflict Resolution* 44 (2): 228–49.

Esteban, J., and D. Ray. 2011. "Linking Conflict to Inequality and Polarization." *American Economic Review* 101: 1345–74.

Esteban, J., L. Mayoral, and D. Ray. 2012. "Ethnicity and Conflict: An Empirical Study." *American Economic Review* 102 (4): 1310–42.

Fearon, J. 2004. "Why Do Some Civil Wars Last So Much Longer Than Others?" *Journal of Peace Research* 41 (3): 275–301.

Fearon, J., and D. Laitin. 2003. "Ethnicity, Insurgency, and Civil War." *American Political Science Review* 97 (1): 75–90.

Femia, F., and C. Werrell. 2012. "Syria: Climate Change, Drought and Social Unrest." The Center for Climate and Security, February 29.

Gershenson, D. 2002. "Sanctions and Civil Conflict." *Economica* 69 (274): 185–206.

Gleditsch, K. 2007. "Transnational Dimensions of Civil War." *Journal of Peace Research* 44 (3): 293–309.

Gleditsch, K., and K. Beardsley. 2004. "Nosy Neighbors: Third-Party Actors in Central American Conflicts." *Journal of Conflict Resolution* 48 (3): 379–402.

Gurr, T. R. 1970. *Why Men Rebel.* Princeton, NJ: Princeton University Press.

Hassine, N. 2014. "Income Inequality in the Arab Region." *World Development* 66: 532–56.

Kanbur, R., and A. Venables, eds. 2005. *Spatial Inequality and Development.* Oxford: Oxford University Press.

Kaufmann, D., A. Kraay, and M. Mastruzzi. 2010. "The Worldwide Governance Indicators: Methodology and Analytical Issues." Policy Research Working Paper 5430, World Bank, Washington, DC.

Khalifa Isaac, S. 2015. "Gulf Assistance Funds Post-2011: Allocation, Motivation and Influence." Strategic Sectors: Economy and Territory. Panorama. *IEMed. Mediterranean Yearbook 2016.*

Kiendrebeogo, Y., and E. Ianchovichina. 2016. "Who Supports Violent Extremism in Developing Countries? Analysis of Attitudes Based on Value Surveys." Policy Research Working Paper 7691, World Bank, Washington, DC.

Lake, D., and D. Rothchild. 1998. *The International Spread of Ethnic Conflict: Fear, Diffusion, and Escalation.* Princeton, NJ: Princeton University Press.

Lipton, M. 1977. *Why Poor People Stay Poor: Urban Bias in World Development.* Cambridge, MA: Harvard University Press.

Lynch, M. 2016. *The New Arab Wars: Uprisings and Anarchy in the Middle East.* New York: Public Affairs.

McLauchlin, T. 2010. "Loyalty Strategies and Military Defection in Rebellion." *Comparative Politics* 42 (3): 333–50.

McNulty, M. 1999. "Media Ethnicization and the International Response to War and Genocide in Rwanda." In *The Media of Conflict: War Reporting and Representations of Ethnic Violence,* edited by Tim Allen and Jean Seaton. Chicago: University of Chicago Press.

Montalvo, Jose, and Marta Reynal-Querol. 2005. "Ethnic Polarization, Potential Conflict, and Civil Wars." *American Economic Review* 95 (3): 796–816.

Murshed, M. 2009. "Conflict as the Absence of Contract." *Economics of Peace and Security Journal* 4 (1): 32–38.

Ostby, G. 2008. "Polarization, Horizontal Inequalities and Violent Conflict." *Journal of Peace Research* 45 (2): 143–62.

Ostby, G., R. Nordas, and J. Rod. 2009. "Regional Inequalities and Civil Conflict in Sub-Saharan Africa." *International Studies Quarterly* 53: 301–24.

Regan, P. 2000. *Civil Wars and Foreign Powers: Interventions and Intrastate Conflict.* Ann Arbor, MI: University of Michigan Press.

———. 2010. "Interventions into Civil Wars: A Retrospective Survey with Prospective Ideas." *Civil Wars* 12 (4): 456–76.

Stewart, F. 2000. "Crisis Prevention: Tackling Horizontal Inequalities." *Oxford Development Studies* 28 (3): 245–62.

———. 2002. "Horizontal Inequalities: A Neglected Dimension of Development." Queen Elizabeth House Working Paper 81, University of Oxford.

Tilly, C. 1978. *From Mobilization to Revolution.* Reading, MA: Addison-Wesley.

Walter, B. 1997. "The Critical Barrier to Civil War Settlement." *International Organization* 51 (3): 335–64.

Williamson, S., and C. Abadeer. 2014. "Protest, Uprising and Regime Change in the Arab Spring." *Muftah*, January 28.

World Bank. 2011. *Middle East and North Africa: Investing for Growth and Jobs.* Economic Developments and Prospects Report. Washington, DC: World Bank.

———. 2017. *World Development Report 2017: Governance and the Law.* Washington, DC: World Bank.

CHAPTER 8

Development Consequences and Policy Implications

Development Consequences

The civil wars in Iraq, Libya, the Syrian Arab Republic, and the Republic of Yemen erased years of development progress and inflicted widespread suffering, internal displacement, and external migration on a scale not seen since World War II. In several countries, state services collapsed and large areas fell under the control of terrorist groups. Syria's civil war led to the most dramatic collapse, marked by widespread destruction, hundreds of thousands killed or disabled, and millions driven away from their homes.[1]

The post–Arab Spring wars impoverished millions of Arab people and made them dependent on humanitarian assistance. Estimates suggest that the poverty rates in Syria surpassed 80 percent in 2015,[2] but refugees, nearly half of them children, also live in dire conditions. Poverty rates among refugees in Jordan and Lebanon were estimated to be about 70 percent in 2014 (Verme et al. 2016). Because many refugees have not been able to obtain work permits, they have either remained unemployed or at the mercy of employers in the informal sector, where most of them work with no protection, on an irregular basis, and for low wages. Child and maternal mortality skyrocketed, and life expectancy slumped as thousands of people died either directly from violence or indirectly from hunger, neglect, and lack of health services and medications (Ianchovichina 2016). The health of the population and the skills of the workforce declined significantly in war-torn countries as access to services deteriorated and the quality of these services worsened, unemployment rates rose, and real wages declined, especially for unskilled workers. The wars forced millions of children out of school because many schools were destroyed, closed their doors, or were turned into shelters for the internally displaced (Devarajan and Mottaghi 2016). A large share of these children have lost years of schooling, while children in the territories occupied by terrorist groups such as the Islamic State of Iraq and Syria (ISIS) have been scarred for life by harsh military training, exposure to violence, and ideological indoctrination.

The burden on poor communities throughout the Middle East has been heavy given that the majority of refugees and internally displaced people relocated to the poorest parts of the region. By the beginning of 2016 close to 20 million people were displaced by the post–Arab Spring civil wars in the region, according to estimates by Devarajan and Mottaghi (2016), who use data from the UN High Commissioner for Refugees and the International Organization for Migration (IOM). The majority of the displaced people moved to safer parts of their own countries, but about one-third of the displaced sought refuge in neighboring countries in the Middle East and North Africa (MENA) and Europe. Turkey absorbed the largest absolute number of refugees, but the concentration of refugees has been highest in Lebanon and Jordan. Outside the Levant, a large number of Libyans escaped to Tunisia, and many Yemenis sought shelter in Djibouti. Many young refugees have been unable to attend school or make academic progress because of overcrowded classrooms, persistent economic hardship, or language barriers (for example, in Turkey).

The civil wars in the post–Arab Spring period have been associated with economic collapses in the war-torn countries and significant spillover effects in neighboring economies. Growth in other developing MENA countries slowed down substantially because of political instability, the threat of terrorism, and war-related spillover effects as well as external challenges linked to the economic slowdown in European and emerging markets. In many countries inflation soared, tourism collapsed, investment plummeted, and the state's ability to finance public services was eroded as governments increased spending on national security at the expense of productive investments in public services and infrastructure. Thus, the socioeconomic performance of the developing MENA region has deteriorated significantly since 2011. Annual economic growth more than halved, on average, in real terms and dropped to nearly zero in per capita terms (figure 8.1).

Sadly, the Arab Spring, which started with calls for fairness and improvements to standards of living, has led to a drastic drop in the quality of life throughout the region and devastation and hardship in war-torn Arab states. Since 2010, dissatisfaction rates have continued to rise, especially in war-torn and war-affected economies (figure 8.2). Meanwhile, government actions have largely failed to address the popular grievances voiced during the Arab Spring demonstrations. Little progress has been made with reforms that would effectively deal with corruption and elite capture. The major structural impediments that stifled private sector

FIGURE 8.1

Reversal of Fortunes in Developing MENA

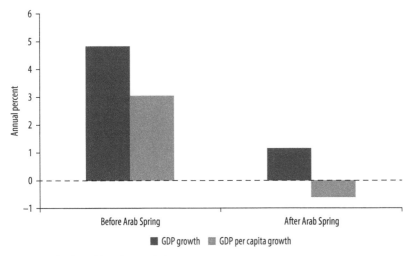

Source: World Bank, World Development Indicators.
Note: GDP = gross domestic product; MENA = Middle East and North Africa. "Before Arab Spring" covers the period from 2005 to 2010; "After Arab Spring" covers the period from 2011 to 2014.

FIGURE 8.2

Rates of Suffering in Arab Economies

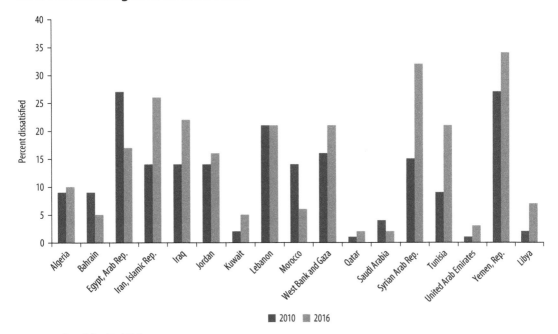

Source: Data from Gallup World Poll.
Note: Dissatisfaction is measured using Cantril Ladder scores. People with a score of 4 or below are classified here as dissatisfied.

growth before the Arab Spring remained intact, although some governments made progress toward renewing the social contract.

Several external shocks worsened the situation even in the richest countries in the region and accelerated the need for macroeconomic adjustment. In mid-2015, oil prices plunged to levels unseen since the early 2000s. In response, the Gulf Cooperation Council (GCC) countries had to quickly moderate the level of redistribution domestically and regionally. They tightened fiscal policy, tapped into their foreign reserves, and turned to debt markets to finance their deficits (Devarajan et al. 2016). About $88 billion in sovereign bonds or government-related enterprise debt was issued to fill the gap in GCC budget deficits. In Saudi Arabia, authorities turned to taxation to raise revenues. They introduced a tax on undeveloped land, airport fees for foreigners, a value added tax (VAT), and additional taxes on tobacco and soft drinks. They also reduced subsidies and raised the prices of fuel, gas, and water. In Kuwait, gasoline prices were partially deregulated, electricity and water tariff hikes were approved, and a VAT was proposed along with privatization of state-owned oil service companies. Fiscal consolidation in the United Arab Emirates included electricity and water price increases and reductions in fuel subsidies and capital transfers to government-related entities. Qatar's authorities started rationalizing subsidies and developing new revenue sources. In Oman, the government aimed to improve the fiscal accounts by implementing fuel subsidy reform and cuts in defense and capital spending as well as in wages and benefits; removing some tax exemptions; increasing corporate income taxes, excises, and fees for government services; and levying a VAT. Bahrain made significant fiscal consolidation efforts by significantly raising gasoline prices; removing subsidies on energy, water, and some types of food; and implementing revenue-enhancing measures such as increasing tobacco and alcohol taxes and government services fees.

Realization that a low-oil-price environment may persist long term compelled GCC authorities to start implementing reforms in line with renewing the social contract. The Saudi government announced Vision 2030 and the National Transformation Program in the second quarter of 2016. The plan effectively launched a renewal of the social contract, aimed at revamping the scope of public investments, strengthening the private sector and its role as an engine of growth, and reducing subsidies. Along with these reforms, the government started implementing reforms to improve transparency and government efficiency. Kuwait announced its 2015–2019 Development Plan in support of non-oil private sector growth. Bahrain proposed to privatize several state-owned businesses, and Oman approved an economic diversification program that supports sectors such as manufacturing, tourism, and logistics.

Slow growth in Europe and the increased incidence of terrorist acts hit the economies, particularly the tourism sectors, of most developing Arab countries, with grave results for investment and jobs. The spillover effects of the Syrian conflict tested the stability of neighboring countries and strained their fiscal accounts, making the implementation of difficult macroeconomic adjustment policies an urgent priority. Following delays in the implementation of important fiscal reforms, Egypt is set to resume its fiscal consolidation plans, which include energy subsidy reform, measures to curb the growth in civil servant wages, improved tax collection, and implementation of a VAT. Exchange rate liberalization is expected to improve competitiveness, but also to increase inflation and hardship among the poor and vulnerable. In Tunisia, a new national unity government is expected to unlock the political bottlenecks to economic reforms and implement measures to strengthen security and improve the business environment. Sustained fiscal consolidation since 2013 and the fall in oil prices helped reduce the twin deficits in Morocco. In Jordan, containing the fiscal deficit and implementing the latest International Monetary Fund program is expected to be challenging given the size of the adjustment, the scope of structural reforms, and the security challenges in Jordan and neighboring countries.

Overall, the macroeconomic deterioration suggests that the cracks in the old social contract have grown bigger and renewing the social contract in the region has become imperative. However, the reforms that are part of this renewal will pose new challenges. Mounting social discontent from government spending cuts, tax hikes, rising youth unemployment, and erosion in living standards indicates that governments cannot simply turn off redistribution without implementing meaningful reforms to strengthen private sector growth and social transfers for the poorest and most needy citizens and to improve the quality and inclusiveness of governance institutions. Failure to address these needs will place the stability and security of these countries at risk.

A new social contract implies the need for a new and inclusive governance model for security. Drawing on the lessons from this study, the next section describe the contours of a new social contract and a new governance model for security in the MENA region.

Toward a New Social Contract and Governance Model

This study's main objective is to provide empirical evidence on the root causes for the Arab Spring protests and the post–Arab Spring civil wars and to nourish the debate on future reforms. The diagnostics presented in this study suggest that it was not high economic inequality but a broken social contract that led to the Arab Spring. Under the old social contract, in place for half a century, development outcomes were positive but not sustainable. The model relied on redistribution through a large and inefficient public sector in exchange for limited voice and accountability. The private sector's growth was weakened by distortions and elite capture that protected the rents of connected businesses but limited opportunities for investment and the growth of firms that did not have connections to the ruling elites. An important observation is that the system was perceived to be unfair because many people felt excluded and were angered about the "relative deprivation" between the people with connections to the ruling elites and those without connections.

In many developing Arab countries, weak growth meant growing deficits, which limited the ability of governments to expand public employment and improve the quality of public services. Eventually the old social contract led to widespread dissatisfaction and a middle-class squeeze, with frustration running particularly high among the relatively young, educated, middle-class urban residents, who were dissatisfied with their living standards and the pervasive corruption in the forms of nepotism and cronyism. Although education and health care were free and energy and water were subsidized, the quality of these services was so poor that many people resorted to the private sector for them. Redistribution through subsidies could not address these people's quests for more and better jobs and for more equitable opportunities. As the social contract broke down, the premium on freedom increased, creating demand for political and economic change.

Developments since the Arab Spring revealed cracks in the old social contract in all Arab countries, although to different extents. Therefore, all Arab states need to work toward replacing the old social contract with a new one. The new social contract must rely on a strong private sector, supported by an efficient government that is accountable to citizens for quality service delivery and that regulates enterprises evenhandedly. Governments in oil-rich countries will have to improve the efficiency of institutions managing oil wealth and invest oil rents efficiently and equitably into physical capital and intangible assets, such as institutions and skills. As pointed out by Gill et al. (2014), policies for inclusive economic growth appear to work only when they are supported by efforts to diversify economies' asset portfolios across the main types of assets: natural resources, physical capital, and intangible capital. The need for rebalancing asset portfolios has gained urgency since 2014 when oil prices plunged as has the need to create jobs for the large number of young people joining the labor force every year.

After decades of state dominance and exclusion, citizens must be empowered to become active participants in the private economy. To empower private entrepreneurship, governments must demonstrate commitment to business-friendly reforms that lower the costs of doing business, reduce complex regulations protecting the rents of connected firms, and ensure unbiased application of the law. Strategic public investments made by the state must complement—not compete and crowd out—private investors. The role of citizens must also change as individuals become active participants in the private economy and social safety nets are targeted to those living in extreme poverty.

Building inclusive institutions will be crucial for the success of the new social contract, and it will pay off in economic growth and shared prosperity. According to Wallis (2011, 48), "impersonality—treating everyone the same without regard to their individual identity—ranks near the top of good institutional outcomes in the pantheon of growth theory." Therefore, the new governance model for security will have to be based on a balanced mix of inclusive institutions that create incentives for cooperation among different stakeholders, fair dispute settlement, redistributive policies that support the most needy people, and rule-of-law institutions that protect and respect the rights of all citizens.

The empirical evidence in this study suggests that all countries in the region are vulnerable to civil unrest, albeit to different extents. The cracks in their old social contracts and security models are bigger in countries with larger twin deficits, weaker governance institutions for security, and overlapping divisions along regional, ethnic, or sectarian lines. In these countries there is an urgent need to renew the social contract and concurrently work to rebalance governance institutions toward greater inclusion. The growing polarization must be countered with vigorous efforts to develop institutions and policies that work for all citizens. Otherwise, true prosperity and stability in the region will remain elusive, and the region will continue to be shaken by popular anger.

Notes

1. The Syrian war and the spread of the Islamic State of Iraq and Syria (ISIS) have cost the Levant region an estimated $35 billion in lost output just during the three-year period since mid-2011 (Ianchovichina and Ivanic 2016).
2. UN-backed report by the Syrian Center for Policy Research (2015).

References

Devarajan, S., and L. Mottaghi. 2016. "The Economic Effects of War and Peace." *MENA Quarterly Economic Brief*, World Bank, Washington, DC.

Devarajan, S., Q. Do, A. Brockmeyer, C. Joubert, K. Bhatia, and M. Abdel-Jelil. 2016. "Economic Perspectives on Violent Extremism." *Middle East and North Africa Economic Monitor*, October, World Bank, Washington, DC.

Gill, I., I. Izvorski, W. van Eeghen, and D. de Rosa. 2014. *Diversified Development: Making the Most of Natural Resources in Eurasia*. Washington, DC: World Bank.

Ianchovichina, E. 2016. "Economic Costs of Post-Arab-Spring Civil Wars in the Middle East and North Africa." Strategic Sectors: Economy and Territory. Panorama. *IEMed. Mediterranean Yearbook 2016*.

Ianchovichina, E., and M. Ivanic. 2016. "Economic Effects of the Syrian War and the Spread of the Islamic State on the Levant." *World Economy* 39 (10): 1584–627.

Syrian Center for Policy Research. 2015. *Syria: Alienation and Violence, Impact of the Syria Crisis Report 2014*. Damascus, Syria: Syrian Center for Policy Research.

Verme, P., C. Gigliarano, C. Wieser, K. Hedlund, M. Petzoldt, and M. Santacroce. 2016. *The Welfare of Syrian Refugees: Evidence from Jordan and Lebanon*. Washington, DC: World Bank.

Wallis, J. 2011. "Institutions, Organizations, Impersonality, and Interests: The Dynamics of Institutions." *Journal of Economic Behavior and Organization* 79: 48–64.